RANGERS
A MATCH TO REMEMBER

RANGERS

A MATCH TO REMEMBER

DAVID MASON

MAINSTREAM
PUBLISHING
EDINBURGH AND LONDON

First published in Great Britain in 2001 by
MAINSTREAM PUBLISHING COMPANY (EDINBURGH) LTD
7 Albany Street
Edinburgh EH1 3UG

ISBN 1 84018 545 7

A catalogue record for this book is available from the British Library

Typeset in Caslon and Gill
Printed and bound in Great Britain by
Mackays of Chatham

CONTENTS

DAVIE WILSON

Davie Wilson broke through to the Rangers first team in 1957, just as the last remnants of Bill Struth's side were disappearing. Sharing the outside-left position with Johnny Hubbard in the first few years, he was to eventually make the number 11 jersey his own in 1960. From then he remained almost a permanent fixture in the Rangers side for four solid seasons, until the up-and-coming Willie Johnston took over.

Always a fans' favourite, he was synonymous with the success that Scot Symon's team experienced in the late '50s and early '60s. With Alex Scott then Willie Henderson on the right flank and Wilson on the left, there was no other team in Scotland with such power on the flanks. Fast and direct, Wilson was a classical winger and he had an incredible knack for winning penalty kicks. It was often said that if he was tackled on the halfway-line, he would still end up tumbling in the penalty area!

One of the great Rangers legends, Wilson played over 370 games for the club scoring 155 goals on the way. In a glittering career, he won four Scottish Championships, five Scottish Cup and two League Cup winner's medals. He also earned 22 caps for Scotland.

SCOTTISH FIRST DIVISION CHAMPIONSHIP
FALKIRK 1 (Duchart) RANGERS 7 (Wilson 6, Scott)
Attendance: 18,000
Brockville Park, Falkirk — 17 March 1962

FALKIRK: Whigham; Rae, Hunter; Thomson, Milne, Pierson;
Wilson, Harrower, Oliver, Duchart and Tulloch.
RANGERS: Ritchie; Shearer, Caldow; Millar, Davis, Baxter;
Scott, McMillan, Wilson, Brand and Henderson.

Ritchie, Shearer, Caldow; Greig, McKinnon, Baxter; Henderson, McMillan, Millar, Brand and Wilson. Even thirty-odd years on, that great side has a magic ring to it, particularly to the forty-somethings who were reared in the era when manager Scot Symon's Rangers dominated Scottish football. Those days are long past, but many of that team maintain their association with the club today, some hosting the various corporate functions that have become an integral part of the modern Ibrox.

Davie Wilson has played his part in hosting, deep in the heart of the corporate areas of the stadium, but nowadays he can more often be found among the ordinary fans who once revered him as a true Ibrox hero. Looking as fit now as he did when he romped up and down the pitch in the number 11 jersey, he still gets a tingle of excitement when he comes to Ibrox and is still fondly remembered by most who had the pleasure of seeing him storm up the left wing. Strangely, however, he is also often remembered for his performance in a position that he was quite unaccustomed to. The occasion was the annual Home International clash between Scotland and England. The year was 1963 and the venue was Wembley Stadium.

Wilson played at his usual position on the left flank but, early in the match, the Scots full-back and Wilson's Ibrox colleague, Eric Caldow, suffered a tragic leg-break. With no substitutes allowed at that time, Wilson was switched to the left-back spot as the ten-man Scots soldiered on. Wilson was immense as Scotland, inspired by Jim Baxter, went on to record a famous victory over the Auld Enemy.

Wilson won 22 caps for Scotland but, curiously, neither that famous Wembley match nor any other appearance for the national side features as his match to remember. Instead, Wilson reflected on a game watched by just 18,000 fans at the humble surroundings of Brockville Park, Falkirk. Ordinarily, a League match at the home of the local 'Bairns' would hardly seem like the setting for a game that was destined to be the highlight in the career of a Rangers legend. But that fine day in 1962, Wilson scored a record six goals in a 7–1 victory for the Light Blues. He recalls the match vividly.

'I was switched to centre-forward that day because Doug Baillie was ruled out through injury and Jimmy Millar was switched back into the half-back line. I had played in that position before and Scot Symon knew I could score goals, so he probably reckoned that I would fit in fine. Alex Scott played on the right wing and a young Willie Henderson took the number 11 jersey for the day. Symon was a great man and knew the game outside in, although he never had a tracksuit in his life. He knew how to motivate players, what they could do, and he had great faith that his players could play the game off the cuff. We played with each other so many times that we developed a great understanding.

'We used to work out moves together and had a bit of a laugh at times too, on and off the field. I remember one incident in a match against Hibernian at Easter Road when we were awarded a penalty. Jimmy Millar walked up to place the ball on the spot then strolled back as if he was preparing to take it. I ran forward and scored while the keeper, Ronnie Simpson, was standing with his arms by his side. "What's happening here?" he said to the referee. "It's a goal. Read about it in the paper in the morning, son!" replied the ref.

'Anyway, when the game kicked off at Brockville, there was a full house of just under 20,000 inside the ground, including my father who went to every match. It was a ground that I liked, and I had some happy memories of the place. I even recall going there as a youngster and being passed over the heads to the front so that I could see the game and get a close view of my Rangers heroes.

'The crowd also included the Falkirk chairman, Duncan Ogilvie, and his family. They were personal friends, but at the end of the game Duncan's daughter could hardly bring herself to look at me. I had scored a barrowload of goals that destroyed her team!

'It was just one of those days. I scored three goals with my left foot and three with the right. I even had a goal disallowed near the end because Alex Scott was in an offside position. Strangely, it was only 1–0 at half-time, although I scored four in a 15-minute spell just after the break. My last goal came less than ten minutes from the end and that caused a problem for the Saturday evening sports papers. I think it was the *Green Citizen* that concluded my scoring at five and carried the headline – *"Wilson Goes Nap!"*.

'After the game Mr Ogilvie gave me the ball, a white, laced, leather ball, which I still have. I might have been a better header of the ball if it didn't have that lace!

'Today I am the proud chairman of the "Six Goal Club"! We only have one other member – Dixie Deans. He is the vice-chairman,' laughed Wilson. 'I was really hoping that Marco Negri would get a sixth goal against Dundee United in that remarkable performance early in season 1997–98, because our wee club is crying out for members!'

Whether there will ever be any more members of the 'Six Goal Club' is uncertain. Then again, if anyone does aspire to this elite club he would probably be a striker. It shouldn't be forgotten that Wilson's natural berth was on the left wing. Within a few days of that match at Brockville, Wilson continued on the goal trail, scoring a hat-trick for the Scottish League in a 4–1 victory over the English League.

Millar regained his number 9 jersey for the next Rangers match but, ironically, he never scored again that season. Next season, though, Wilson and Millar scored 77 goals between them. And then there was Brand – he added another 40 goals! Millar, Brand and Wilson – doesn't that just take you back?

AT THAT TIME

Russia made headline news as the Sputnik soared into orbit, giving the Soviets a lead over the United States in the space race.

Top television shows at the time included *Cheyenne* on STV, with the popular *Captain Pugwash* entertaining younger viewers on the BBC.

In football, Billy Wright was appointed manager of Arsenal at a salary of £3,000 per year.

In Scotland, there was a tug-of-war over Ian McColl's contract as Scotland boss.

For smokers, a box of 20 Churchman's Olympic cigarettes cost two shillings and ten pence.

For those interested in holidays, you could buy a caravan for just over £400.

Davie Wilson scores in a match against Kilmarnock at Ibrox, watched by Jim Forrest and Killie's Frank Beattie.

ANDY GORAM

Known simply as 'The Goalie', Andy Goram was arguably the best keeper to represent Rangers in the post-war era. Signed initially as part of Walter Smith's overhaul of the side, reducing the number of foreign players in the wake of UEFA restrictions for European competition, he quickly established himself as an idol at Ibrox. Goalkeepers rarely get the opportunity to display emotion, but Goram was different. His enthusiasm for the game, and more particularly Rangers, was never in doubt. He was the rock upon which Rangers' success under Walter Smith was built.

Signed in 1991, he went on to play over 250 games for the club and recorded over 100 shut-outs. A key member of the victorious side that won 'Nine-in-a-Row', his collection of medals included six Scottish Championships, three Scottish Cups and two League Cups.

He was also one of the best post-war keepers to represent Scotland, earning 43 caps. When he left Rangers in 1998, as Walter Smith's side disbanded, he played for a number of provincial sides and also had a short spell under Alex Ferguson at Manchester United. However, his name will always be synonymous with that great Rangers side of the '90s.

SCOTTISH PREMIER LEAGUE CHAMPIONSHIP
CELTIC 0 RANGERS 1 (Laudrup)
Attendance: 50,041
Celtic Park, Glasgow — 14 November 1996

CELTIC: Kerr; Boyd, O'Neil (McKinlay), McNamara, Stubbs, Grant, Di Canio, Wieghorst, van Hooijdonk, Thom (Cadete) and Donnelly.
RANGERS: Goram; Cleland, Robertson, Gough, Petric, Bjorklund, Moore, Gascoigne, McInnes (van Vossen), Albertz and Laudrup.

Few players have embraced the institution that is Rangers more than Andy Goram, although his attachment to the club developed long after he first embarked on life as a professional footballer. 'The Goalie' was hardly what you could call a born and bred 'Gers man, although football, and goalkeeping in particular, was in his blood. His father had played between the sticks for a number of clubs, including Hibernian, and once faced Rangers at Ibrox.

When Goram senior moved south and set up the family home in Bury, the family connections with Scotland appeared all but lost. The young Andrew Goram was born and raised in Lancashire, and continued the family interest in sport. He became a fine young cricketer, but it was on the football field, in goal, that he came to the attention of England's professional sides. Oldham were eventually to lure him to Boundary Park, where he remained for six seasons and also earned international recognition with Scotland.

In 1987, drawn by his bloodline affinity with Scotland, he returned along the trail his father had taken 40 years earlier by joining Hibernian. Goram flourished at Easter Road, consolidating his reputation as a solid, dependable keeper. There was little prospect of him ending up at Ibrox during his early years in the Premier League, as Souness' revolution was well under way, with the popular Chris Woods holding the number 1 jersey. By the time Walter Smith took over the reins, however, the increasing restrictions on foreign players in European competitions forced the new Rangers manager to reappraise his squad.

In 1991, therefore, Goram earned a dream move to Ibrox for a fee of around £1 million, as Woods returned south, a victim of the UEFA rules governing the European competitions. It looked a sound move for Rangers, although few expected that Goram would provide any added strength to the side. At the time some even felt that he might prove to be inferior to Woods. Seven years on, however, any doubters had been proved wildly wrong as Goram emerged to be recognised as one of the Rangers greats.

During those seven seasons he became a cornerstone in the success of Walter Smith's side, and was an influential figure in the club's successful completion of the much-vaunted 'Nine-in-a-Row' sequence.

The final six Championships were won with Goram in harness, although he virtually sat out one season when knee ligament damage curtailed his appearances. Three Scottish Cup and two League Cup medals were added to his collection, in a great Ibrox career.

13

Having played in most of the club's memorable games during the '90s, I suspected that he might have difficulty selecting any specific game, although, knowing his ever-intense desire to beat Celtic, I expected that he would choose an Old Firm match – I wasn't to be disappointed.

'The game that I remember most vividly and brings a smile to my face is the second League clash of season 1996–97 with Celtic at Parkhead. It was a great game from a Rangers perspective, and it was one of my best performances for them.'

Rangers went into the match behind their rivals on goal difference. Just seven minutes into the match, however, they took the lead through Brian Laudrup, who drilled the ball past Kerr after a slip by young Celtic defender Brian O'Neil. Throughout the match, Rangers looked comfortable under Celtic pressure, and they were lethal in counter-attack.

The Light Blues had several opportunities to increase their lead, first through a Gascoigne penalty, saved by Kerr; next, with an empty net beckoning, van Vossen had a shocking miss. With the game apparently secure, Rangers were then shocked when, with only eight minutes left, the referee ruled that Richard Gough had tripped Simon Donnelly inside the box. Celtic striker Pierre van Hooijdonk stepped forward.

Goram recalls, 'I had been involved in a few clashes with van Hooijdonk earlier in the game and was unhappy with his performance to say the least. I had made a few good saves, but I was gutted at the prospect of us losing points when we had done so well in the game. I had watched him taking penalties before, but really, in these situations, you just pick a side and take a chance. He hit it low and hard to my right. I dived and turned it around the post. I was elated and I think it showed in my reaction! I shouted to Hooijdonk, but I won't repeat what I said!'

It was a vital save for Rangers, as they went on to take the points and a lead in the Championship they were not to surrender. For Goram there was time for reflection after the game. 'I just thought how it was every schoolboy's dream to play in a big match and, as a keeper, to save a penalty in these circumstances was wonderful. It is a game and a feeling that will always be with me.'

By the end of the season Rangers had secured Championship number eight – 'One more to go', the fans sang. Goram helped Rangers to that glorious ninth while Celtic boss, Tommy Burns, rued the contribution of 'The Goalie' in killing off his own side's challenge. 'Put it on my headstone,' he said, 'Andy Goram broke my heart.'

For Goram, in beating Celtic, victory was never sweeter.

AT THAT TIME

Prince Charles celebrated his 48th birthday with Camilla Parker-Bowles at Highgrove.

Meanwhile, Michael Jackson married mum-to-be Debbie Rowe in Australia.

On television, 17 million viewers tuned in to see Raquel split from Curly Watts in *Coronation Street*.

In the cinema, *Independence Day* was still drawing crowds to the new Showcase Complex at Uddingston.

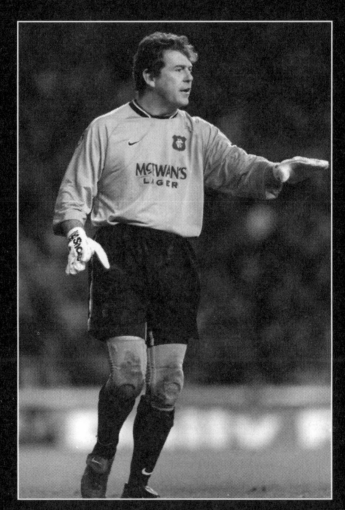

Andy Goram in action.

BRIAN LAUDRUP

A career that took him from his Danish homeland to the Bundesliga in Germany and then the Italian Seria A, eventually led Brian Laudrup to Ibrox Stadium, where he blossomed in front of an adoring Rangers crowd. He was signed for a fee of £2.5 million from Fiorentina after the Italian dream soured: he and other foreign players became a focus of fans' disappointment when the Tuscany side failed to impress. Rangers benefited, gaining a player who was not only determined to get his career back on track, but who was also keen to find a stable setting for his family. He found it in Scotland.

His time with Rangers was arguably the best of his career. It provided the platform for excellent performances at club level, which he carried onto the international stage. Rarely has the game seen such a talented footballer with sublime skills that enthralled fans everywhere. He was the pivotal figure in the closing stages of Rangers' quest for 'Nine-in-a-Row', going on to seal the decisive Championship with crucial goals at Celtic Park and then in the clincher against Dundee United at Tannadice Park. Laudrup's efforts earned him three Scottish Championships, one Scottish Cup and one League Cup winner's medals. He gained deserved recognition as the Scottish Player of the Year in successive seasons in 1995 and 1996, voted for by both the Scottish Football Writers' Association and his fellow professionals.

He also won 82 caps with Denmark and was a member of their victorious side that took the 1992 European Championship in Sweden. His departure from Rangers for Chelsea in 1998 was greeted with universal disappointment and it never really worked out for the Dane at Stamford Bridge. He later moved to Ajax then back to Copenhagen, but injury ended his career prematurely. He retains a close affinity with Rangers and still makes occasional trips to his second homeland at Ibrox and Scotland.

SCOTTISH PREMIER LEAGUE CHAMPIONSHIP
DUNDEE UNITED 0 RANGERS 1 (Laudrup)
Attendance: 12,000
Tannadice Park, Dundee – 7 May 1997

DUNDEE UNITED: Dykstra; McInally, McKimmie, Pressley, Perry; Pedersen,
Olofsson, Zetterlund (Dolan), McSwegan, McKinnon and McLaren (Winters).
RANGERS: Dibble; Cleland, Robertson; Petric, McLaren, Bjorklund,
Moore, Gascoigne (McInnes), Durie, Miller and Laudrup (McCoist).

By the time the 25-year-old Brian Laudrup arrived at Ibrox in July 1994, he was more widely travelled and had achieved considerably more than most seasoned pros. After quitting local Danish side Brondby, where he had been from the age of six, Laudrup left home to ply his trade in Germany. A successful spell with Bayer Uerdingen prompted a move to Bayern Munich at a record transfer fee of £2 million. It was a fine spell for Laudrup, who flourished in the Bundesliga, going on to be voted Best Foreign Player.

At just 23, he was already a big name in football, and a year after joining Bayern he reached a real milestone in his international career. Conflict in Yugoslavia forced the beleaguered nation to withdraw from the 1992 European Championships and Denmark stepped into the breach. In keeping with the best of Hans Christian Andersen's fairy tales, the Danes grasped the opportunity that had seemed lost to them and provided the shock of the tournament by surging to take the trophy with a 2–0 win over Germany. Brian and his brother Michael were key members of that victorious side.

These were glorious years for Laudrup, but more sobering times were just around the corner in what he called 'the worst years of my life'. An ill-fated £3.5 million transfer to Fiorentina opened the door to the glamour of the much-lauded Serie A, but also to a fanaticism the young Dane was quite unprepared for. In contrast to the glory years at Bayern and on the international stage, Laudrup found the Tuscany side in a sorry state. As Fiorentina struggled, so did Laudrup, and the frenzied fans turned on the very players they should have acclaimed. Laudrup said, 'I was desperate, I simply had to leave that club.' Ultimately, through fear, he sent his family home. Not even a loan deal to AC Milan could alter Laudrup's perspective of life in the Serie A.

Alert to Laudrup's enthusiasm for change, Rangers manager Walter Smith explored the possibility of the player's transfer to Ibrox. Laudrup thought over the move very carefully, eager to ensure that Scotland and Rangers could satisfy not just his career interests, but also those of his family. When he finally agreed to join the Light Blues, he wooed the fans by announcing that 'this is the one club I've been looking for, for my family. Now that we've got this club we are all happy.'

Happy he might have been, but he still had to show the Rangers fans that he was worthy of the number 11 jersey that had been worn by a succession of illustrious predecessors, including Wilson, Johnston, Cooper, and Walters. In his first match, ironically a pre-season friendly against Italian side Sampdoria at Ibrox, Laudrup provided more than a glimpse of the magic that would characterise his time at Rangers.

Championships and cups followed, but most significantly Laudrup helped edge Rangers towards the Holy Grail that was 'Nine-in-a-Row'. In a Rangers career that saw him play over 150 first-class games, Laudrup was in little doubt as to his most memorable match.

'It has just got to be the "Nine-in-a-Row" clincher at Tannadice,' he said. 'Although we had won at Parkhead just a few days earlier and everyone had virtually ruled out Celtic's chances of catching us, I was conscious that we could still lose it. We were also aware just how much it meant to the fans to equal Celtic's record. Quite simply, we couldn't think about losing.'

Injury had affected Laudrup's displays through the campaign, but if ever there was a time when Rangers needed the Dane's inspirational qualities and flair it was in the perilous United ground in Dundee's Tannadice Street. Late in the first half Charlie Miller surged down the left wing and sent a swinging cross ball into the United area. Laudrup arrived on cue to deliver the ball beyond the clutches of keeper, Dykstra, into the net.

'It was a wonderful feeling scoring that goal. I hardly ever scored goals with my head, even in training, but here I had managed to get perhaps the most important goal of my career. It was very emotional, especially when the final whistle went and we knew that "Nine-in-a-Row" was finally ours.'

At the end of the season Laudrup decided to move on before the persuasive powers of David Murray encouraged him to see out the remaining year of his contract at Ibrox, in the face of a sizeable bid from Ajax to take the 'Great Dane' to Holland. Laudrup's final year was punctuated by illness and injury and he suffered the ultimate disappointment of a barren season. At the end of his contract he became part of the mass exodus as Smith's side was scattered to the four winds.

He headed off for a short-lived spell at Chelsea, before his career turned full circle with a return to Denmark where it all began. Occasionally he returns to Ibrox, attracted by the sheer magnetism of Rangers. 'Home from home,' he calls it.

Inevitably, when he appears in the crowd it is quite an emotional experience. 'There's only one Brian Laudrup,' the fans still sing, rising en masse around him in the crowd. They reflect on his contribution to a great era and that memorable evening in Dundee. It was a night to remember for a true Ibrox great.

AT THAT TIME

In the news, Princess Diana admitted that she was still haunted by the eating disorder bulimia.

In politics, Donald Dewar had just been elected Secretary of State for Scotland and set out his plans for the future of the country.

In the cinema, *Anaconda* scared audiences throughout the country, while on television, Kevin Webster and Sally exposed their marriage split on *Coronation Street*.

In football, Alex Ferguson prepared to take Manchester United to their fifth title while Schalke recorded a 1–0 win in the first leg of the UEFA Cup final against Inter Milan.

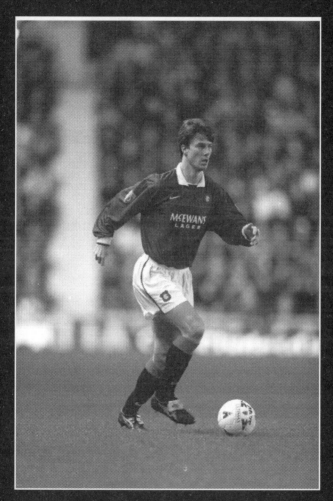

Brian Laudrup showing typical poise
in action for Rangers.

DAVIE PROVAN

After the conclusion of Eric Caldow's career at Ibrox, Rangers produced another fine full-back who, like his predecessor, would also go on to play for Scotland. Davie Provan was just 18 when he broke through to the Rangers first team under Scot Symon in 1958. However, it was 1963 before he achieved a regular place in the side, after serious injury to Caldow created the opportunity at left-back that he had longed for. For four seasons he made the number 3 jersey his own, enjoying the glorious times in the final years before the great Rangers side of the '60s waned, and also experiencing the disappointments when Celtic re-emerged under Jock Stein.

The highlight of his career was undoubtedly in season 1963–64 when he helped the club to the Treble. It was a glorious spell for the big defender, who earned his first cap in 1964 and went on to appear five times for Scotland. When he left Rangers in 1970, he had a spell in England with Crystal Palace and Plymouth Argyle, before returning to Scotland to play for St Mirren. After a short stint as manager of Albion Rovers, he returned as chief scout under John Greig. Now he assists at Ibrox in match day entertainment, but he will always be best remembered for his glorious Rangers career.

SCOTTISH CUP FINAL
RANGERS 1 (Brand) CELTIC 1 (Murdoch)
Attendance: 129,527
Hampden Park, Glasgow — 4 May 1963

RANGERS: Ritchie; Shearer, Provan; Greig, McKinnon, Baxter;
Henderson, McLean, Miller, Brand and Wilson
CELTIC: Haffey; Mackay, Kennedy; McNamee, McNeill, Price;
Johnstone, Murdoch, Hughes, Divers and Brogan

Rangers star of the '60s, full-back Davie Provan played over 260 first-class games for the club in a career which brought him a League Championship medal, three Scottish Cup and two League Cup emblems. He also earned four Scotland caps and played in the European Cup Winners' Cup final of 1967. So why, he often wonders, do young kids still come up to bait him about the hard time that Celtic's Jimmy Johnstone gave him when the pair faced each other in Old Firm clashes?

It is a source of amusement nowadays for the likeable Provan, but there were times when it really grated because he had a fair amount of success against the diminutive Celtic winger. One match in particular came readily to mind as he delved into the memory banks to recall the stirring encounters with 'Jinky'.

'The Scottish Cup final of 1963 was certainly my most memorable match because just four weeks earlier I was playing reserve-team football and the left-back berth was held by Eric Caldow,' recalled Provan. 'The programming of the Home International fixtures in these days was strange, with Scotland scheduled to meet England at Wembley in April, a full seven weeks before the end of the domestic season. Eric was selected for the national side, but tragedy hit him early in the game when he suffered a broken leg. With Caldow clearly ruled out for the season, I was drafted in for a League game against Hibs at Ibrox, which we won comfortably.

'A few days later we met Dundee United in the semi-final of the Cup and trounced them 5–2. I had a good game and settled into the side. We played a few more League matches before the Cup final beckoned and I faced the prospect of my first Old Firm game against one of the best wingers in the game. Naturally I was a bit tense, but looked forward to the occasion immensely.

'In those days there was no special preparation for a game of that magnitude, and we simply turned up at St Enoch's ready for the trip to Hampden. As expected, I retained my place in the side, but I was nervous in the run-up to the kick-off. I tended to be like that before most games, but this one was something special. We knew there would be around 120,000 at the game.

'When the match kicked off the nerves disappeared, and I knew that my role was to stop Johnstone. As we came face to face there was a fair amount of chat as we tried to wind each other up. That was to become fairly typical of my encounters with him.

'As the game progressed, I felt that I had him under control and he was pretty ineffectual. Late in the first half, Ralph Brand opened the scoring for us, but Murdoch grabbed an equaliser just before half-time. We had the upper hand for most of the game, but their keeper, Haffey, was having one of those days. The game ended with the score at 1–1, and the match was scheduled for replay 11 days later. It would have been played that midweek, but another international, against Austria, interrupted the card.

'Once again, there was a massive crowd at Hampden for the replay [120,000], but this time Johnstone was dropped. I took a lot of satisfaction from that because it showed that I had done my job against him in the first game. Celtic brought in Bobby Craig, from Sheffield Wednesday I think, in place of Johnstone, but I had won the psychological battle.'

An early goal from Brand set the pattern of the match, and Davie Wilson added another just before the break. Midway through the second half, Brand grabbed a third and Rangers began to play around with their old rivals as the clock moved towards presentation time.

When the final whistle went, there was immense joy for Provan in winning his first Cup final, and the realisation that he had secured his place in the side. There would be many more battles with 'Jinky', but for the present, the honours lay with the Rangers number 3. 'It was a big game for me,' recalled Provan, 'but not one that Johnstone would want to remember.'

It was not always that way, as the kids now remind him, but who cares? Today he has happy memories of some great times at Rangers, and he probably doesn't realise that in 24 games against Celtic, he was on the losing side only six times. That included five wins out of five in the following season 1963–64, which is the kind of ratio every Rangers fan would savour. In contrast, Jimmy Johnstone would not welcome recollection of that ratio – or for the most part his encounters with Provan.

AT THAT TIME

An Irish steamer en route to Belfast was turned back to Glasgow when rioting broke out among Old Firm fans after the match.

Popular television programmes at the time included *Perry Mason, Double Your Money,* and *The Lucy Show,* which was top in the ratings.

There were some big blockbuster movies showing in Glasgow cinemas, led by

Lawrence of Arabia, starring Peter O'Toole, which was on at the Gaumont Cinema.

A rare appearance on stage from Sammy Davis Jnr enthralled a Glasgow audience at the Odeon Theatre in Renfield Street.

In football, Rangers were top of the Scottish First Division, and Everton held first place in England.

Chelsea, Newcastle United, Sunderland and Leeds United all contested the English Second Division title.

Davie Provan (centre) with teammates Davie Wilson (left) and
Ronnie McKinnon (right) at a private function.

ERIC CALDOW

Eric Caldow joined Rangers in 1952 from Ayrshire schools' football, after serving a spell with Muirkirk Juniors. As William Struth's penultimate signing, he was fortunate to be reared among legends such as Young, Cox, Woodburn and Waddell, but he too would go on to reach such status. He is generally regarded as one of the finest full-backs produced, not only by Rangers, but by Scotland, captaining both. In an international career, which was cruelly ended by injury at Wembley, where he sustained a broken leg in 1963, he earned 40 caps and the distinction of being the first Rangers player to play in the World Cup finals. A poll of readers of a national tabloid newspaper conducted in 2000 voted him the greatest left-back to have served his country.

By the time his career at Ibrox ended in 1966, he had played over 400 first-class matches, winning five League Championships, two Scottish Cups and three League Cups. He also led Rangers to their first European Cup Winners' Cup final and helped to build Rangers' name in continental football through the '50s and early '60s.

Rangers through and through, Caldow is now one of a group of former players who assist on match days at Ibrox, hosting the many corporate functions in the stadium. Each Saturday is now a trip down memory lane not only for the popular Caldow, but also for the many fans who remember his great service in a Rangers jersey.

SCOTTISH CHAMPIONSHIP FIRST DIVISION
RANGERS 2 (Matthew, Caldow) CELTIC 1 (Peacock)
Attendance: 55,000
Ibrox Stadium, Glasgow — 1 January 1959

RANGERS: Niven; Shearer, Caldow; McColl, Telfer, Stevenson; Scott, McMillan, Murray, Brand and Matthew.
CELTIC: Beattie; McKay, Mochan; Smith, Evans, Peacock; McVittie, Jackson, Colrain, Divers and Auld.

Players who have played in a Rangers v Celtic clash invariably go dewy-eyed at the mere mention of the fixture, but Eric Caldow has more reason than most to be nostalgic about Old Firm matches. Not only did he play 39 times in the fixture, losing on only 10 occasions, he was pitched into a League clash between the sides just a week after making his first team début. Injury had ruled out George Young from taking his usual right-back berth, but Bill Struth had no hesitation about blooding the 18-year-old Caldow alongside the likes of McColl, Woodburn, Cox and several other household names of the period.

It was a memorable game for Caldow as the Light Blues went on to win 2–1, but it was not this game that remains most vivid in his mind. He recalled, 'I loved to play in these games, but there is one match that particularly comes to mind among all the rest because I scored the winner!

'It took place on New Year's Day 1959. I remember that we had no special preparations for the match other than to avoid the festivities of Hogmanay. We hoped that there would be plenty time for a drink and a celebration after the game.

'We assembled at the St Enoch Hotel for a pre-match meal. I always had something light – a plate of feathers!' he joked. 'Then we headed off to Ibrox where Scot Symon would read out the team about an hour before the game. In the dressing-room, the jerseys were already hanging on the pegs. I remember when I first arrived at Ibrox I wondered if everyone was ten feet tall, because the pegs were so high that you had to stand on the benches to reach them.

'There was no pre-match tactic talk – Scot Symon wasn't that kind of manager. He just picked the team and then expected us to get on with it. I think that the crowd was over 50,000 and I remember that the weather was deplorable, with rain and sleet making conditions very heavy.

'Celtic got the opening goal early in the first half through Peacock, but Andy Matthew pulled us level minutes afterwards. The game looked to be drifting to a draw and, as time went by in the second half, the lines on the pitch were beginning to disappear. At that time the referee was duty bound to abandon a match if the lines weren't obvious.

'With only 25 minutes to go, Alex Scott hit a speculative shot and Celtic's Neilly Mochan armed it away. The referee had no hesitation in awarding us the penalty and I stepped forward to take it. Celtic's Bobby Evans edged over to the penalty spot and, while the referee was looking elsewhere, he scuffed away at the ground to obliterate the mark. I firmly

believe that he was trying to get the game abandoned, but the referee was having none of it.

'I stepped forward and scored, but that wasn't the end of the drama,' said Eric. 'With only five minutes left, Celtic were awarded a penalty and Bertie Auld searched desperately for the spot. They found it, but he then proceeded to blast the ball off the bar and it was cleared. The game ended in a 2–1 win for us. After the game we headed back to the hotel where our delayed celebrations began in earnest. We may even have been celebrating a possible Championship win because it was generally recognised that the team that was leading at the turn of the year would win the title.'

In fact, Rangers did go on to win the Championship that season and Celtic finished in lowly sixth place. It was certainly a match to remember for the Rangers contingent and one to forget for the Celts. But then, that tended to be the way of things in Caldow's era!

AT THAT TIME

The world watched as rebel leader Fidel Castro enforced his grip on Cuba by taking control of the capital Havana as the country's former rulers fled.

For those looking for some Spanish sunshine, a flight to Palma from Renfrew airport was priced at 59 guineas (approx. £61.95). For those more interested in a 12-day bus tour of the Basque coast, the cost was 52 guineas (approx. £54.60).

In the cinema, *South Pacific* was showing at the Gaumont in Sauchiehall Street, with *Tom Thumb* enthralling audiences at the ABC Coliseum in Eglinton Street.

In football, Rangers were shocked by a transfer request from South African star Johnny Hubbard.

Glasgow's boxing star, Peter Keenan, announced his intention to retire after losing a European title fight.

Eric Caldow in action for the Light Blues.

WILLIE HENDERSON

Ask any fan to nominate the best number 11 to grace the Rangers blue jersey and the likes of Cooper, Laudrup, Wilson and even Morton will feature amongst the illustrious nominees. But ask them to select the greatest number 7 and, almost to a man, they will nominate Willie Henderson. He broke into the Rangers first team in 1961 at the tender age of 17, and within 18 months a series of superlative performances thrust him into the Scotland side.

He went on to wear the dark blue of Scotland 29 times in a period when the jersey was contested by Celtic's Jimmy Johnstone. They each had a claim on the position, but, while Johnstone offered tanner ba' skills, Henderson was pacy and much more direct.

Diminutive in stature at just 5 ft 4 in., he had the heart of a lion and became an influential member of Scot Symon's great side of the early '60s. In an Ibrox career spanning 12 years, he celebrated two Championships, four Scottish Cup victories and two League Cup successes. Nowadays, he joins many of his contemporaries in hosting events in the Ibrox corporate suites, reliving memories of great times past.

SCOTTISH CUP FINAL
RANGERS 3 (Millar 2, Brand) DUNDEE 1 (Cameron)
Attendance: 120,982
Hampden Park, Glasgow — 25 April 1964

RANGERS: Ritchie; Shearer, Provan; Greig, McKinnon, Baxter; Henderson, McLean, Millar, Brand and Wilson.
DUNDEE: Slater; Hamilton, Cox; Seith, Ryden, Stuart; Penman, Cousin, Cameron, Gilzean and Robertson.

31

Matches become memorable for a whole range of reasons, often for the glint of silverware, individual performance, or personal circumstances quite unrelated to the game itself. In Willie Henderson's case, one match stands above all others as memorable for a combination of all these reasons.

'The 1964 Scottish Cup final carries so many memories for me and so much emotion,' he said. 'It was emotional as much for what was happening off the park at that time as on it.'

Henderson's memories carried him to a momentous clash with Dundee in the nation's showcase Scottish Cup final. It was a period when Scot Symon's team was at its peak. Having won the League Cup, and with the Championship also in the bag, the Treble looked a distinct possibility. However, Dundee would be no pushovers, they were a formidable side with some great players, including Hamilton, Cox, Gilzean and Andy Penman, who would eventually end up at Ibrox. In goal, they had a fine keeper named Bert Slater.

Rangers' route to the final included a 2–0 win over Celtic in the fourth round, with Henderson scoring the vital second goal just after the interval. However, the earlier games were forgotten as Rangers turned their attention to the final. Henderson recalled, 'Two weeks before the game we had beaten England 1–0 at Hampden and I was on a high. But any elation I felt after that was shattered when I got word that my father had suffered a serious brain injury at work. The doctors reckoned it was touch and go whether he would pull through. I had this constantly preying on my mind as we prepared for the final at Hampden.

'When we got to Hampden I was conscious that a victory would maybe give my father a bit of a lift, so I was determined to do well. I have got to say that I felt under enormous pressure. The crowd inside the stadium was officially just over 120,000, but I thought there was even more. The game kicked off and was exciting with us having the upper hand through most off it, but being continually thwarted by Bert Slater in the Dundee goal. Indeed, many people called it the "Slater Final" after the game.

'The game was level without a goal at half-time, and the deadlock wasn't broken until 19 minutes from the end. I sent a corner over and Jimmy Millar got on the end of it. Our celebrations with the crowd were short-lived, however, as Dundee equalised just a minute later with a goal from nowhere, and the game looked really deadlocked.

'With time running out, I called to an ambulance man sitting at the side of the park to let me know how the clock stood. He told me there were four minutes left and I remember thinking to myself that it was time something was done! By this time, Davie Wilson and I had switched wings. We would often do that to create openings. I took the ball from Jim Baxter, then jinked up to the line before floating the ball into the penalty area. Millar again got to it and nodded the ball into the net. The Rangers end erupted with a deafening noise. We were naturally delighted and knew we were on our way to the Cup. Within a minute I broke away again and this time my cross was first met by Davie Wilson, whose shot was beaten out to Ralph Brand. Ralphie turned on the rebound to hit it into the net for the third goal.

'As the final whistle blew, I just broke down in tears. There was just so much emotion in that game, considering the circumstances surrounding my father, the occasion of the Cup final and the drama of these last few minutes.

'After the walk up the steps to collect the silverware, we ran around the pitch with the Cup on the traditional lap of honour – one of the last teams to do so in Scotland incidentally. [In later years, the SFA ruled that teams should only go to their own fans to avoid crowd trouble.]

'Right after the match, I shot up to Edinburgh Royal Infirmary, clutching my medal tightly in my hand. My father was very ill, but I believe the victory did help to lift him. He never worked again, but he did eventually recover well enough to enjoy a few good years afterwards. To many people that game was all about winning the Cup and securing the Treble, but it meant so much more to me.

'It is a game that will always linger with me – a real match to remember.'

AT THAT TIME

In football, Liverpool became champions in England for the sixth time in their history.

Walter McGowan headed the other sports news with the story of his unsuccessful defence of his European flyweight title at the hands of Italian Salvatore Burrunni.

In the cinema, *Dr Strangelove* was greeted with rave reviews when it showed at the

Odeon. Meanwhile, in the Coliseum Cinerama, the wraparound screen showed *How The West Was Won* to startling effect.

Aussie singer Frank Ifield made an appearance at the Odeon Theatre.

While the Rangers fans celebrated their Cup win, they were disappointed to learn that Jim Baxter had turned down terms for the next season.

On the World front, Scots soldiers were flown into Aden to counter attacks from mountain guerrilla fighters.

Willie Henderson in action for Rangers.

ALEX WILLOUGHBY

There were not many glimpses of light amidst the gloom that descended on Ibrox in the aftermath of the infamous Scottish Cup first-round defeat that Berwick Rangers inflicted on Rangers in 1967. However, two young players offered some promise for the future to the chastened supporters. One, Sandy Jardine, made his first-team début in the first game following the defeat and went on to become a Rangers legend in his own right. The other was Alex Willoughby, who had previously never been seen as anything more than a fringe player.

Ironically, Willoughby's introduction to the team came at the expense of his cousin Jim Forrest who, along with George McLean, was singled out as a scapegoat for the result that sent shockwaves reverberating throughout football.

Willoughby grasped his chance and helped restore Rangers' pride with a remarkable twelve goals in five games. He saw out the remainder of the season in the number 8 jersey and then shared the inside-right berth next season with Andy Penman. When he left Ibrox in 1969, he had played almost 100 first-class games for the side, scoring a remarkable 47 goals. The pinnacle of his career was a League Cup win in season 1963–64 in which he scored one of Rangers' five goals against Morton.

That old time-worn cliché of playing for the jersey was invented to describe players like Alex Willoughby – a real True Blue.

SCOTTISH FIRST DIVISION CHAMPIONSHIP
MOTHERWELL 1 (McCallum) RANGERS 5 (Willoughby 4, A. Smith)
Attendance: 25,000
Fir Park, Motherwell – 4 March 1967

MOTHERWELL: Wylie; Whiteford, R. McCallum; Campbell, Martis,
W. McCallum; Lindsay, Murray, Deans, Cairney and Hunter.
RANGERS: Martin; Johansen, Provan; Jardine, McKinnon, Greig; Henderson,
Willoughby, A. Smith, D. Smith and Wilson.

The worst result in our history' was how manager Scot Symon described Rangers' first-round defeat in the Scottish Cup to Berwick Rangers. Inside-forward Alex Willoughby played for the reserves that day and was in the Ibrox dressing-room when the news of the result from Berwick's little Shielfield Park filtered through. Willoughby had just returned to action after a five-week lay-off through an Achilles tendon injury, which robbed him of the chance to stake a claim for the number 8 jersey.

There was a stunned silence inside the portals of Ibrox when the realisation hit that the score flashes on the radio were no hoax. David Francey, the famous voice of football on BBC radio, relayed the news that most fans could hardly believe, and the majority were destined never to forget.

Alex Willoughby recalled the events vividly. 'I remember the match for a whole range of reasons,' he said. 'My cousin, Jim Forrest, was a scapegoat for that defeat, along with George McLean. Chairman John Lawrence stated in the next Ibrox match programme that Jim would never again kick a ball for Rangers! He was true to his word because Jim was sold off to Preston North End two months later.

'On the Monday after the Berwick match, I was pulled aside by Scot Symon and told that I would be back in the first team on Saturday. That came as quite a shock because it was unheard of for the team to be selected so early. I told him that I was surprised that he was letting me know so early in the week because it wasn't the way he had usually done things. I will never forget his reply. He said that it wasn't his team, but that I was in the side nevertheless.'

Willoughby duly took his place in the side against Hearts at Ibrox, and completely justified his selection with a hat-trick in front of a loyal crowd of over 33,000. He followed that performance with another hat-trick five days later against Clyde, then grabbed a goal a few days later to steal the points for Rangers at Kilmarnock.

A couple of weeks later, he kept up the momentum against Real Saragossa, grabbing the first goal in a 2–0 victory in front of 65,000 fans. Willoughby remembered, 'What a night that was. We had all four seasons on the one evening: it started off as a lovely sunny evening, before the rain, sleet, then lightning came in.'

The weather was more settled by the weekend, however, when Rangers were due to play Motherwell at Fir Park in what was to become Alex Willoughby's match to remember. But if the skies were more settled, the Lanarkshire side were quite unprepared for the tornado that was Willoughby. The fair-haired inside-forward scored four times in a 5–1 win in front of a lock-out crowd in a match that secured Rangers' position at the top of the League.

It was the culmination of a sparkling run of form that consolidated Willoughby's position as a favourite of the fans. 'The Fir Park match was one in which just about everything went right for me and I really felt part of it all. Sadly, Jim Forrest left the club a couple of weeks later, but Berwick was behind him. Ironically, it sparked off the best period I had at Rangers.'

A week after the Motherwell match, Rangers travelled to Spain for the second leg match against Saragossa, and Willoughby, inevitably, again figured, helping Rangers to go through, albeit on the toss of a coin. 'That was a great result for us because they had some great players and many people had tipped them for the trophy. But, it was a wonderful time for me, although the storm crowds were already brewing for Scot Symon.

'It was sad because we really had solid support from the fans, but I have no doubts that the board wanted him out. They eventually did dismiss him less than a year after Berwick.'

It is rather ironic that Willoughby's best time at Rangers was born in the midst of so much drama surrounding the Berwick defeat and its aftermath. However, if there was ever any player who could show the fans that things move on, it was him – quite simply because he could so easily have been one of the adoring fans who turned up faithfully week after week through these troubled times.

AT THAT TIME

Sandie Shaw was voted Britain's representative in the Eurovision Song Contest and later went on to win the competition.

The Beatles topped the charts with 'Penny Lane', pushing Engelbert Humperdink into second spot.

In theatre, Jimmy Logan, Ronnie Corbett and Lonnie Donegan shared top billing in the Alhambra.

On television, *Take Your Pick* continued to remain popular on STV, with *Jackanory* and *Crackerjack* entertaining younger viewers on the BBC.

In football, Manchester United were leaders in the English First Division.

A floodlit Ibrox on European night against Real Saragossa.

JONATHAN WATSON

He may never have played football at any reasonable level, but he has been Graeme Souness, Denis Law, Kenny Dalglish, Ossie Ardiles and more – or at least it seems that way. Jonathan Watson is the star of BBC's *Only An Excuse*, and his caricatures of the game's biggest names have had television and stage audiences rolling about with laughter. None enjoy the various take-offs of Scotland's heroes more than the great men themselves, and, Watson once stood in front of the Rangers players on the eve of a major match, delivering a pre-match talk of sorts. He may not have been Walter Smith, but he certainly sounded like him, and the famous blue cardigan just added to the character.

It is no surprise that much of his act has focused on the Old Firm because they provide fertile ground for entertainers with talent like Watson. It helps too that he is a True Blue and, when his busy television and theatre schedule permits, he can be found on a match day in his seat in the Club Deck at Ibrox.

The closest Watson came to representing Rangers was in his superb performance in the club's stage play *Follow, Follow*, which opened in the King's Theatre, Glasgow, in 1993. A major television name before then, Watson's success has continued ever since with various acting roles, including continuation of the *Only An Excuse* format that has proved so successful. It now forms a traditional part of the BBC's Hogmanay schedule.

Souness, Law, and Dalglish – he sounds like each of them. Now if that could be translated to his feet – what a player we would have!

RANGERS I (McCoist) CELTIC 0
Attendance: 45,191
Hampden Park, Glasgow — 31 March 1992

RANGERS: Goram; Stevens, Gough, Brown, Robertson; Gordon,
Spackman, McCall, Huistra; McCoist and Durrant.
CELTIC: Marshall; Morris, O'Neil, Mowbray, Whyte,
Boyd; Miller, McStay, Collins, Nicholas and Creaney.

Jonathan Watson was like every youngster who fell under the magical spell of Rangers, desperately wishing that he could play with the club. Although small in stature, that was unlikely to be a hindrance because Rangers has had its fair share of diminutive figures who have gone on to make their mark in the club's history. Willie Henderson and Tommy McLean come immediately to mind, but, like the vast majority of young Bears, Watson's dream was never to be fulfilled.

However, if he was destined never to impress on the field, he certainly made up for it on the stage, where he has made as great an impact on the game as many who pulled on a jersey. Nowadays, he can count several of the stars he has taken off as friends. It has also helped him to develop a close association with the club, attending many club functions and performing in his inimitable way.

Like every fan, Johnny never tires of talking about football and the great games he has seen. 'Yes, I've seen some memorable matches and Rangers' win over Juventus in 1978 stands out among them. That was a wonderful victory because many of the Juve side played for the Italian national side. I also remember Rangers 3–2 win over Celtic in 1986, just after Graeme Souness' appointment as manager was announced. Ally McCoist scored a hat-trick and, although it wasn't the biggest of tournaments, the result was of immense importance to the fans and the new regime.

'That was a wonderful evening, but the game that really sticks out in my mind as a match full of drama and excitement was that great night in 1992 when Rangers beat Celtic 1–0 in the Scottish Cup semi-final.

'I sat right in amongst the Bears and I remember we were stunned when referee Andrew Waddell produced the red card for Rangers left-back David Robertson in the opening minutes after he flattened Celtic winger Joe Miller.'

Robertson later told of being instructed by Rangers boss Walter Smith to put in a heavy tackle on Miller early on. Smith had reasoned that Miller might not have the enthusiasm for a physical game if Robertson tackled hard in the opening minutes. The Rangers defender's tackle, a crude body-check after just six minutes, was certainly illegal, and probably not what Smith had intended, but it may not have warranted Robertson's dismissal. Watson recalled, 'I didn't get a clear view of it, but it did seem harsh at the time and we were in for an anxious time with almost the full 90 minutes ahead.

'Then, just when Celtic were getting the upper hand, we really turned the tables on them. I think it was around midway through the first half when Rangers broke forward and Ally McCoist struck with a superb goal, sweeping the ball into the net from the edge of the box. We were delirious and, even though the rain teemed down, we were happy, though still conscious of Celtic's man advantage.

'They put us under extreme pressure through the second half, but our defending on the night was incredible. We had Richard Gough and John Brown at the heart of the defence and I loved that pairing. But what struck me most was the attitude of the side. There was a real determination that typified what we had come to expect of Rangers. That famous word *character*, used so often by Jock Wallace, came to mind as I watched them defy everything that Celtic could throw at them.'

Rangers went on to lift the Scottish Cup with a 2–1 win over Airdrie, and that determination, allied to tremendous skill, saw the Light Blues clean up the following season on the domestic front with the Treble. In fact, that year, Rangers almost made it to the Champions Cup final, ultimately losing out to Marseilles despite remaining undefeated through the tournament. The competition, and in particular the away contest with the French champions, was also memorable to Watson for another reason. He joined Rangers on the team flight to the match and addressed the players just prior to the game, removing some of the tension from a match that would be one of their biggest of the decade.

Rangers fought back that evening to secure a point after losing the opener to Marseilles, highlighting the character that Walter Smith had instilled in the team – a spirit that had been evident that cold and victorious night in Hampden Park a year earlier.

AT THAT TIME

Britain prepared for a General Election on 9 April and the polls showed that Labour Leader Neil Kinnock had a 7 per cent lead in the race to Downing Street. In Hollywood, Anthony Hopkins celebrated winning an Oscar for Best Actor for his role in *The Silence of the Lambs*.

On television, *Blockbusters* was a hit with all ages and *Only Fools and Horses* continued in a repeat series.

For motor enthusiasts, Mitsubishi launched their latest Colt hatchback at a price starting from £8,600.

In football, Celtic's beseiged board signed a pact of unity with promises for the future, while in England, Tottenham's Gordon Durie prepared to face West Ham.

(Left to right) Maurice Johnston, Terry Butcher, Scott Nisbet, Richard Gough, Jonathan Watson, and Ally McCoist.

ANDY CAMERON

While many entertainers carefully hide their allegiance in a city where football is divisive, popular actor/comedian Andy Cameron has never been afraid to pin his colours to his chest. Indeed, just like the great Lex McLean before him, Cameron has embraced his love for Rangers within an act that never offends, but reflects the great humour that lies deep within the city. If the club was ever to appoint a court jester, then Cameron's name would be at the forefront of candidates.

Born in London in 1940, Cameron decided that his future did not lie in the industrial blacklands of Glasgow, but in front of the footlights of the theatre. He first rose to prominence in the unlikeliest circumstances with a song, 'Ally's Tartan Army' in celebration of Scotland's ill-fated World Cup sojourn to Argentina in 1978. The song reached the top ten in the UK charts and Cameron made an appearance on BBC's *Top of the Pops*. More television work followed, alongside regular appearances on stage throughout Scotland. Showing versatility, he extended his repertoire to serious acting with a role in STV's serial soap opera, *High Road*. However, Andy Cameron is best known and loved for his humour.

EUROPEAN CUP — SECOND ROUND, SECOND LEG
PSV EINDHOVEN 2 (Lubse, Deijkers) RANGERS 3 (MacDonald, Johnstone, Russell)
Attendance: 28,000
Eindhoven, Holland — 1 November 1978

PSV EINDHOVEN: Van Engelen; Krijgh, Stevens; van Kraay, Brandts,
W. Van der Kerkhof, Jansen, Poortvliet, R. Van der Kerkhof, Lubse and Deijkers.
RANGERS: McCloy, Jardine, A. Forsyth; T. Forsyth, Johnstone,
A. MacDonald, McLean, Russell, Parlane, Smith and Watson.

A ndy Cameron is a loyal True Blue who has shared every emotion as a Rangers fan over the last 40 years. He has celebrated in the golden days of the early Scot Symon era, with the likes of Baxter, Millar, Henderson, Wilson and Greig, and mourned through the lean years of Celtic's 'Nine-in-a-Row', before the catharsis of Rangers' very own 'Nine' in the '90s brought sunshine back to Ibrox again.

Over that period he has seen many memorable matches, but there was one in particular that remained vivid in his mind. 'Rangers v PSV Eindhoven in 1978 – what a match that was,' he said with eyes alight.

'I remember we drew the first game 0–0 at Ibrox, and few expected us to progress as we went to Holland for the return leg. In fact, I met a few of the press guys in a pub before the game. Hugh Taylor, Jimmy Sanderson, and Archie McPherson were all there, and they had written Rangers off. Loyal to the cause, I defended our boys and bet each of them a drink that we would go through.

'So, off I went, bunnet, scarf and all, to spread the gospel of the 'Gers to the good people of Eindhoven, in hope if not in expectation. I remember the Bears were in good spirits and fine voice. Remembering that any crowd trouble could put us out of Europe, irrespective of anything that happened on the field, manager John Greig came over to thank us for our support, but also to remind us to be on our best behaviour. He received a resounding cheer before he headed off to the dugout.

'The scene was set, the Dutch equivalent of Bovril was hot and we settled into our places for the kick-off. No sooner had we started up another defiant chorus than we got off to a nightmare of a start. With only 34 seconds gone, the Dutch champions scored to put us behind in the tie. I suppose it must have been the excitement, or maybe it was the Dutch Bovril, but I made my way quickly to the toilets to gather my thoughts, you could say!

'Then this wee Bear appeared beside me, covered in badges – they were on his scarf, bunnet, jumper, you name it! He was the picture of dejection as he mumbled, "Lucky ********! They scored before we were ready."

'You could just imagine Greigy rushing out to the referee shouting: "Come on ref, we wurny ready!"

'Anyway, we started causing the Dutch a lot of problems on the break and we were up on our feet when "wee Doddie" [Alex MacDonald] grabbed an equaliser early in the second half. PSV scored again a few minutes later, but our guys fought back with a lot of determination and, with 25 minutes left, Derek Johnstone got the equaliser. That put us ahead in the tie on the away goals rule.

'As the minutes ticked away, we knew we were through, but the icing on the cake was still to come. With only three minutes left on the clock, "wee Tam" McLean swept a pass out to Bobby Russell who advanced on the keeper before tucking the ball under his body and into the net.'

Cameron's eyes twinkled at the recollections of one of Rangers' best results in Europe. The return journey was delayed as Eindhoven fell fogbound, but the blue-and-white army were undeterred in their celebrations, with Andy Cameron at the forefront searching out his friends from the press corps. Did he get the drink they promised him for a Rangers win?

'Aye, all in one night, but I think it was worth it!' he laughed.

It was a night to remember for Rangers and Cameron, but in five decades of fervent support there are many more memories that linger, including the Ne'erday game of 1960 when his great hero, Jimmy Millar, scored the only goal in the dying seconds.

'I think it was one of Celtic's Bobby Evans' last games and he was involved in the goal. I remember that he headed the ball clear but that it landed at Stevenson's feet and he lofted the ball back into the path of Jimmy Millar. Millar took the ball in his stride and blasted it past Haffey.

'The Celtic defence complained to the referee that it was offside, or maybe they just weren't ready,' he laughed. 'That was a great game, but it still doesn't compare with that great night in Eindhoven,' he said.

Andy Cameron may tread the footlights to the adoration of his audiences, but there is little doubt that he would give it all up for the chance to wear the Light Blue of Rangers. His stories of Rangers are endless, and who needs a scriptwriter with so many like the Wee Bear of Eindhoven around?

He is at home when he takes his place in the Ibrox crowd among the Rangers support. They are his kind of people and he is their kind of man – a real True Blue.

AT THAT TIME

There were growing concerns as the Shah of Iran faced an uprising led by student masses.

On television, BBC continued its popular war serial *Secret Army*, while on STV, ballet dancer Wayne Sleep performed on *Showtime*.

Petrol was expected to rise by over 5p to 80p per gallon.

President Amin of Uganda asked Prime Minister James Callaghan to mediate in its dispute with Tanzania.

The new Volvo 343 was unveiled and priced at £3,349.

Meanwhile, for financial high-flyers a 'Management Accountant' position was advertised at a salary of £6,250.

In golf, Severiano Ballesteros topped the Order of Merit.

Andy Cameron with Bobby Davro in the Ibrox Trophy Room.

IAN McCOLL

Pull on the blue jersey, win a couple of Championships or so, score some goals and perhaps throw in a few caps. A player may be quite justified in believing he has 'made it' as a Rangers star with that little bundle under his belt, but to achieve legendary status demands more.

How about captaining the side, amassing nearly 600 games for the club, and collecting six titles, five Scottish Cup medals and a couple of League Cup emblems on the way? Pretty impressive stuff, especially when you throw in the 14 Scotland caps and the ultimate honour of managing the national side.

There are few who can boast such credentials, but one, Ian McColl, is every bit the Rangers legend. Signed by William Struth as an 18 year old in 1945, he swiftly graduated to the first team and served a quick apprenticeship alongside the likes of old stagers like Shaw and Gillick, before establishing himself as a regular in one of the best teams produced by the club. The names roll off the tongue of many Rangers fans – Brown, Young, Shaw, McColl, Woodburn and Cox – an 'Iron Curtain' of a defence that was the basis of much of Rangers' success in the early years of the post-war era.

McColl was a vital cog in that well-oiled wheel, making crucial tackles in the middle of the back from his right-half berth, and springing attacks with sweeping passes to Willie Waddell ahead of him on the right wing. An intelligent, inspirational figure, he went on to captain Rangers and carried his leadership skills to the Scotland national side, appointed manager while still registered as a Rangers player. He had a great record as Scotland boss, with 16 wins in 27 matches, before he moved on to manage Sunderland.

His affection for Rangers remains undiminished and nowadays he is a regular attender at Ibrox on match days. He was one of the first names to be entered in Rangers official Hall of Fame.

SCOTTISH CUP FINAL

RANGERS 2 (Millar 2) KILMARNOCK 0
Attendance: 108,017
Hampden Park, Glasgow — 23 April 1960

RANGERS: Niven; Caldow, Little; McColl, Paterson, Stevenson;
Scott, McMillan, Millar, Baird and Wilson.
KILMARNOCK: Brown; Richmond, Watson; Beattie, Toner,
Kennedy; Stewart, McInally, Kerr, Black and Muir.

I t is always an honour to meet true footballing 'greats', especially when they have a host of memories adding colour to the great tapestry that is the history of Rangers Football Club. Ian McColl sat in the directors' box at Ibrox and cast his eyes over the playing field, rekindling memories of the days when he graced that same turf under managers Bill Struth and Scot Symon. It is now over 40 years since he packed away his boots after 15 glorious years at the stadium. If there was ever a testament to his contribution to Rangers, it comes in the countless greetings he invariably receives from the older legions when he now makes his way to Ibrox. They remember him well – a strong right-half. Bill Struth once said of him, 'When McColl tackles you, you stay tackled!'

Nowadays, he and his wife run a smart guest house in Milngavie, but get him on to the subject of football and McColl shows a perception of the modern game that belies his age. All too often players of a bygone age are trapped in a time warp where 2-3-5 are the magic numbers that unlock everything in their mind. The former Rangers player is different – just ask the guys at the golf club. He loves wingers, but he explains why things are so much more difficult now for that dying breed due to the increased tactical awareness of sides.

He is the sort of guy who could keep you going for several hours on endless stories of times past, and you can never tire of hearing his vivid recollections of Rangers in the '40s and '50s. But there was one match that he particularly revered.

'It was virtually the last match I played for Rangers – the Scottish Cup final of 1960,' he recalled. 'Having spent nearly 15 years at the club, during which time I won everything, my career was winding down in season 1959–60 and I couldn't command a regular first-team place. Harold Davis had taken my number 4 jersey, but I could have no complaints after such a good career.

'It wasn't a great season for the club, but we had won through to the Cup final against Kilmarnock, and had a last chance to win some silverware. We did have hopes of European Cup success, but the side lost heavily (6–1) to Eintracht in the first-leg semi-final, just ten days before our trip to Hampden. Harold Davis sustained an injury and he was replaced by Albert Franks in a League match at Motherwell, which we lost, five days before the final.

'I was in the reserves through all of this, but on the Thursday before the big game I read the team sheet for the final on the dressing-room wall. I was in! Scot Symon was very formal in that respect – he didn't tell you, you just read it! Unlike today, where the players go off to prepare, we were told to turn up at the St Enoch Hotel on the Saturday where it would be business as usual.

'I was never really fazed with the big crowd because we were used to it. It was to be a great day for Jimmy Millar who scored two goals, and even a missed penalty from Eric Caldow couldn't give Killie hope of taking the Cup back to Ayrshire. The win gave me my fifth Scottish Cup winner's medal in five appearances – I don't know if anyone else managed that. It also completed three Cup wins in a row for me and I took great satisfaction from that,' he recalled with understandable pride.

'I played a couple more first-team games before the end of the season, but by the following year I had drifted back into the reserves. In October of that year Scotland were scheduled to play Wales in Cardiff and they should have been coached by Andy Beattie, who was also boss of Huddersfield at the time. There was no dedicated Scottish manager at that time. The English felt that they couldn't release Beattie because of his club commitments and the Scotland side had then to travel without a boss. They duly lost and all hell broke loose in the press.

'Two weeks later, I was appointed manager of Scotland while still registered as a Rangers player. I played my last game for the reserves on the day Willie Henderson played his first game for the reserves and that gave me great satisfaction because he was a great player. Within a few months I closed the chapter on my Ibrox career to pursue my duties for the national side.'

In almost five years as Scotland boss, McColl made his mark with some memorable victories, particularly over the Auld Enemy. One notable victory, which is revered among the Tartan Army, came at Wembley in

1963, when a ten-man Scottish side, orchestrated by Jim Baxter, teased and tormented England to a 2–1 defeat.

You could go on about the achievements of Ian McColl because there is little he has not achieved in the game. He is a true Rangers legend in the mould of the finest.

AT THAT TIME

A fire in the main stand at Hampden almost brought tragedy to the Cup final when a lighted cigarette fell between the timber boards and set alight dust and wood.

The country was preparing for the wedding of Princess Margaret and Anthony Armstrong-Jones.

Count Basie and his Orchestra were live on stage for one night at the Odeon Theatre in Renfield Street, while flamboyant pianist Liberace appeared at the Empire.

On television, youngsters enjoyed the *Sooty Show*, while the *Palladium* provided the top family entertainment at weekends.

Rangers and Manchester United were linked with top schoolboy sensation Jim Forrest, who later went to Ibrox.

In England, Burnley, Wolves and Spurs were all contesting the English First Division Championship.

The dapper Ian McColl in civvies.

TOM FORSYTH

Solid, dependable and uncompromising are just three of the adjectives that were used to describe Tom Forsyth when he took his berth in the Ibrox back four through the '70s and early '80s. Part of a side that brought two Trebles to Rangers, Forsyth was signed from Motherwell for £40,000, just four months after that famous European Cup Winners' Cup success in Barcelona in 1972. Forsyth initially found himself in the Rangers midfield before Jock Wallace recognised his strong defensive qualities and moved him into the back four. It was a wonderful transition that brought success to both player and club.

In ten great years at the club, Forsyth won three Championships, four Scottish Cups and two League Cups. He went on to play over 300 games for Rangers and his performances earned him a further 21 caps for Scotland to add to the first he won while at Motherwell. It is probably more than coincidence that Rangers went through a poor spell in the years following Forsyth's premature departure from the game through injury. The big defender was the steel upon which every successful side needs to be constructed and his departure from the game was a sore loss for Rangers.

After a short spell as manager of Dunfermline, he joined Tommy McLean as his assistant manager at Motherwell, before leaving the game altogether. In recent times he has returned to Ibrox along with many of his former teammates, assisting in hosting the corporate suites on match days.

SCOTTISH CUP FINAL

RANGERS 3 (Parlane, Conn, Forsyth) CELTIC 2 (Connolly, Dalglish)

Attendance: 122,714

Hampden Park, Glasgow — 5 May 1973

RANGERS; McCloy; Jardine, Mathieson; Greig, Johnstone, MacDonald;
McLean, Forsyth, Parlane, Conn and Young.
CELTIC: Hunter; McGrain, Brogan (Lennox), Murdoch, McNeill, Connolly;
Johnstone, Deans, Dalglish, Hay and Callaghan.

When legendary Rangers boss Jock Wallace took his players to the tortuous sand dunes of Gullane as part of a strict training programme in the early '70s there were doubters. Critics poured scorn on the intense physical hardship that the players endured, feeling the focus should be more on ball work. But it was all part of the former 'jungle-fighter's' strategy to turn his side into the fittest in the League. He believed it would be the platform for their success.

Quickly, and defiantly, Wallace shaped a resilient, formidable unit that displayed immense character and swept all before it. However, it was a side that possessed more than just supreme fitness, it also had skill in no short measure.

The squad won two Trebles, in 1976 and 1978, and if there was one player that fulfilled all of Wallace's expectations of a Ranger it was Tom Forsyth. The big defender quickly endeared himself to the Ibrox legions as a player who shored up the Rangers back line, leaving the offensive play to the likes of Johnstone, Parlane and Smith. Ironically, however, he is best remembered for a goal that won the Cup for Rangers.

In a career filled with many happy moments, including a famous tackle on England's Mick Channon, which saved a certain goal as Scotland marched to victory over the Auld Enemy at Hampden, Forsyth picked out the 1973 Cup final as his match to remember.

'Yes, that game holds special memories for me, for obvious reasons,' he recalled. The television images of Forsyth racing away with arms outstretched in celebration as the ball lay in the back of the Celtic net are unforgettable. Especially for Forsyth, whose goal after 60 minutes gave Rangers a 3–2 lead that was to prove decisive in a game dubbed the 'Centenary Cup Final' in commemoration of the club's 100-year existence.

'I can remember it all so well. I went upfield for a free-kick and my old teammate Dixie Deans went along to mark me. Tommy McLean swept the ball over in one of these great crosses that he could put in, and Derek Johnstone got in a header. The ball beat Ally Hunter in the Celtic goal, hit the post, and then rolled along the line. I raced in to knock the ball over the line and then set off so fast they could hardly catch me,' he laughed.

'It is every kid's dream to score the winning goal in a Cup final and I was just so elated that I had done it. What made it extra special was the fact that it was my first Cup final. I think there were over 120,000 in the stadium and the atmosphere was amazing.

'The next day just about everybody I knew came around to the house to offer their congratulations. A great week was capped off when I was called into the Scotland squad for the game against England at Wembley. I ended up on the bench, but it was still a good period.'

With 30 minutes to go, some may have feared that Celtic could haul themselves back into the game, and for Forsyth, with a dream outcome at stake, the anxiety could not have been more intense. However, he was unbowed, remaining totally confident that Rangers could hold out. 'I was confident throughout the game that we would win. Even when Celtic opened the scoring through Dalglish in the first half, I sensed we would get back into it. That goal just fired us up and possibly blasted any remnants of nerves because we were quickly back on level terms when Derek Parlane equalised. In fact, I think it was his birthday!'

Alfie Conn put Rangers ahead early in the second half, and Celtic grabbed the equaliser from the spot after John Greig had handled on the goal-line. That set the scene for the dramatic outcome that would put Tom Forsyth's name well to the fore in Scottish Cup folklore. John Greig may have joked later that he knocked the ball in with his studs, but that could not detract from the importance of the goal to Forsyth and Rangers.

The only lingering downside to that wonderful moment is that Forsyth feels that it frequently detracts from his other achievements in the game. 'You would think that all I ever did was score that goal from the reaction I have received since,' but it was clearly a moment to remember.

If ever anyone should doubt his contribution to Rangers, they need only look at his honours and speak to the countless strikers he thwarted with his formidable defensive skills. But then everyone loves a hero, and that sunny day in Hampden Park a Rangers hero was born – living a boyhood dream.

AT THAT TIME

In politics, it was reported that Prime Minister Edward Heath faced a party revolt if he pushed forward further in plans for a Scottish Parliament.

Comedy on television was well served with the likes of *Bless This House* and *Milo O'Shea*. Meanwhile, magician David Nixon opened up with a new show at prime time.

In the charts, Dawn were No. 1 with 'Tie a Yellow Ribbon' followed by Gary Glitter with 'Hello, Hello, I'm Back Again'.

In the United States, worries mounted for President Nixon as the Watergate scandal deepened.

House prices were comparatively cheap with new semi-detached properties in Linlithgow on offer at just under £8,500.

Forsyth scores the winner in the Scottish Cup final, 1973.

SANDY JARDINE

Rangers' shock first-round Scottish Cup defeat by Berwick Rangers in 1967 cast a shadow over Ibrox, but amidst the despair in the aftermath there emerged a youngster who was destined to become one of the finest full-backs to have been produced by club and country. The defeat by Berwick was the catalyst for Jardine's introduction to a Rangers side humiliated by burgeoning criticism. Pitched in for his début against Hearts a week after that notorious defeat, Jardine assisted the rehabilitation with a 5–1 win over the Tynecastle side. He quickly established himself in the side, initially as a half-back, then as a striker, before manager Willie Waddell recognised his potential at full-back.

International honours soon beckoned, culminating in a string of excellent performances in the 1974 World Cup. He attained 38 caps in all and a hatful of medals. They included, three League Championship, five League Cup and five Scottish Cup winner's medals. The pinnacle of his career at club level was, however, Rangers' famous European Cup Winners' Cup success in Barcelona in 1972. He finished his playing career at Hearts, but not before he had achieved his second Player of the Year award – the only player to have achieved the 'double' with awards at two different clubs. Having racked up over 670 first-class games for Rangers between 1967 and 1982, Sandy Jardine is one of the few who could justifiably lay claim to the status of 'Rangers Legend'.

Today, he continues his service to Rangers within the Commercial Department, which brings him into regular contact with corporate guests of the club on match days.

SCOTTISH LEAGUE CUP — THIRD ROUND, FIRST LEG
RANGERS 6 (Smith 3, Johnstone, Miller, MacDonald) ABERDEEN 1 (Davidson)
Attendance: 20,000
Ibrox Stadium — 5 October 1977

RANGERS: Kennedy; Jardine, Miller; Forsyth, Jackson, MacDonald;
McLean, Russell, Johnstone, Smith and Cooper.
ABERDEEN: Clark; Kennedy, McClelland; Robb, Garner, Miller;
Jarvie, Davidson, Harper, Fleming and McMaster.

There was a look of confusion on the face of legendary Ibrox star Sandy Jardine when he pondered over the task of selecting his match to remember. Here was a man who won thirteen domestic medals including ten domestic Cup final victories and two memorable Trebles under the late, great Jock Wallace. It is not easy singling out one memorable game above all others when there have been so many in a long and glittering career.

That famous victory in Barcelona in 1972, when he helped the club to its only European success in the European Cup Winners' Cup, was a definite candidate. It was a victory that was all the sweeter as a 19-year-old Jardine had tasted defeat in the final of that same tournament five years earlier. Or, could there be any tournament more memorable than the 1974 World Cup, when Scotland made a glorious exit, returning undefeated and unbowed, and Jardine was lauded for his performance in the tournament?

Strangely, the one game that Jardine recalled above all others was not one that ended with champagne flowing from a major trophy. 'There is one game that comes to mind, but it wasn't one of these famous matches I have played in,' he recalled.

'It was back in 1977, I think, that we faced Aberdeen in a League Cup tie, just a year after they had trounced us 5–1 in the semi-final of the same competition. They were a good side, with the likes of Willie Miller, Joe Harper and Drew Jarvie in their squad.

'We met them in the first leg of a third-round tie and we were keen to get some revenge. They were a real bogey side to us, and had even beaten us in the first League match of the season.

'Normally, in football, you look to get about eight of your players playing

61

to their potential, but that evening was one of these special times when everyone was bang on form,' he recalled.

'Gordon Smith set us on the goal trail with the opener in the first few minutes. By half-time, Derek Johnstone, Alex Miller and another from Smith put us 4–0 ahead, leaving Aberdeen in tatters. Further goals from Gordon Smith, completing his hat-trick, and Alex MacDonald took our tally to six, with Davidson pulling one back late on for the Dons.'

While Rangers lost the second leg 3–1, it was too little too late for Aberdeen, and the Light Blues progressed to the next round. Indeed, it was to be a significant win for Rangers and Jardine. The success over an Aberdeen side that hitherto had been an obstacle to Rangers provided a platform for the side's fortunes that season. Rangers continued their progress in the tournament all the way to the final where Celtic awaited. A 2–1 victory in extra-time gave Jardine his seventh winner's medal, with the promise of more to come.

While the Dons did exact some revenge for their League Cup hammering, with a 4–0 win in the League, Rangers went on to secure the Premier League Championship. The two sides were poised for one last confrontation in May in the Scottish Cup final. Rangers were looking for a Treble, while the Dons were seeking to salvage something from a season in which they seemed destined to finish second-best to Rangers. It was not to be for Aberdeen, however, as Jardine and his high-flying teammates gave Jock Wallace his second Treble in three years. Not only a match to remember for Jardine, but a whole season.

'Yes, it was a great time for Rangers and me. We had some great players and wonderful team spirit,' he enthused.

Jardine never scored in any of these games against the Dons, but one goal did come to mind that he could scarcely call his most memorable. In fact, he cannot remember a thing about it! 'I scored a wonder goal against Dundee United in a League game in the mid-'70s, I'm told. I took the ball past two defenders then coolly lobbed the ball over Hamish McAlpine. I'm told it was a great goal, but I couldn't remember a thing about it because I was concussed from a clash of heads moments earlier. I suppose it was a wonder I scored at the right end!' he laughed. Memorable for some, but clearly not for Jardine!

It must be near impossible to select a defining moment to savour from a career as illustrious as Jardine's. One thing's for sure, though, in his long and great service to Rangers, he provided more than a few memorable moments for the Light Blue legions who adored him.

AT THAT TIME

The UK car industry was in turmoil with Prime Minister James Callaghan fighting to curb Ford workers' 15 per cent pay demands.

Concorde continued to face opposition from civic groups in New York determined to prevent it landing at Kennedy Airport as concerns of excessive noise mounted.

Honda offered their new Civic model to motorists at a price of £2,140.

The Education Department advertised for secondary school teachers with a starting salary of £2,988.

On television, the *Muppet Show* continued to be popular on ITV with *Anna Karenina* on the BBC.

Sandy Jardine chases down Celtic winger Bobby Lennox in an Old Firm clash.

DEREK JOHNSTONE

It is every schoolboy's dream to score the winning goal in the Cup final, but when that dream is fulfilled at the tender age of 16, in an Old Firm final, the sense of reality must be questioned. But these are exactly the circumstances in which Derek Johnstone burst on to the scene in the 1970, when he was thrown into the League Cup final by Rangers boss Willie Waddell. Johnstone rose above two Celtic defenders to nod in the only goal, with a strike that signalled Rangers' revival after four barren years.

Johnstone had arrived and he became a vital part of the great sides of the '70s that Waddell and then Jock Wallace produced, winning thirteen domestic trophies, including two Trebles and the European Cup Winners' Cup. Exceptional in the air, Johnstone's strength was in his versatility, being as comfortable in the centre of the defence as he was on the front line. But it was in his role as striker that he particularly impressed. In 14 seasons at Ibrox he scored 210 goals in 546 games and were it not for the number of quality players that Scotland had in strike positions through the period he would have added considerably to his 14 caps.

Nowadays, Derek Johnstone is a respected football pundit with regular newspaper features and a place on the gantry for radio match-coverage. With expert commentary laced with no little humour, Johnstone is a popular figure on the airwaves and he leaves no one in any doubt as to his allegiances. However, even opposing fans respect his views. He is remembered as one of the best centre-forwards of the modern era.

SCOTTISH CUP SEMI-FINAL
MOTHERWELL 2 (McLaren, Pettigrew) RANGERS 3 (Miller, Johnstone 2)
Attendance: 48,915
Hampden Park, Glasgow — 31 March 1976

MOTHERWELL: Rennie; W. Watson, Wark; R. Watson, McLaren, Stevens;
McAdam, Pettigrew, Graham, Gardner and Marinello.
RANGERS: McCloy; Miller, Greig; Forsyth, Jackson, MacDonald;
McKean, Hamilton, Henderson, McLean and Johnstone.

For a man who served 14 seasons at Ibrox which included the European Cup Winners' Cup win in Barcelona in 1972 and the great Treble years of the Wallace era, there must be innumerable games that Derek Johnstone remembers with relish. However, one game that remains particularly vivid in the mind of the man they call simply 'DJ' had no silverware at stake and was not fought against any glamorous European side. Instead, it was the semi-final of the Scottish Cup in 1976 against Motherwell.

Johnstone recalled, 'I remember that tie for a number of reasons. We had already won the League Cup with a win over Celtic and we were already ahead in the Championship, so the Treble was definitely on. However, it all started to go wrong not long into the match when Motherwell went two up with goals through Willie Pettigrew and Stuart McLaren. They were two up at the interval and thoroughly deserved their lead.

'Quite simply, we were woeful and didn't look as if we could get back into the game. Then the ball was pumped out of our area and I chased in on goal. Motherwell keeper Rennie came racing out to close me down and I was tumbled inside the box. It was a definite penalty, although the 'Well guys argue about it to this day.

'Alex Miller scored from the spot and that proved to be the turning point in the game, much to the dismay of Motherwell boss Willie McLean and his assistant, Craig Brown.

'We were now on a high and the 'Well defence began to crumble. With ten minutes to go, and Rangers still 2–1 down, Peter McCloy launched one of those kicks that had the ball floating down with ice on it! It bounced just outside the area and I rose to challenge Rennie on the rebound. I got there first and headed it over his head and into the net for the equaliser.'

Johnstone's remarkable transformation of the game was complete when he got on the end of a Greig free-kick to snatch the winner with just two minutes left.

'Motherwell should have won,' confessed DJ, but the victory was so important to us and we went on to win the final against Hearts to secure the Treble. It was to be a good competition for me because I got on the score sheet again in the opening seconds of the final.'

The Treble sealed a first for Derek Johnstone and Jock Wallace, but they were to repeat the achievement two years later with the Rangers striker again playing a prominent role. Again, Motherwell featured in one of the key matches from the campaign that year and Johnstone reflected on a second-half goal spree that turned the game around.

'I remember a game at Fir Park when we were once again two goals down early in the first half, although Gordon Smith and I scored to bring us level at the interval. Manager Jock Wallace gave us a real roasting at half-time and pointed out that we should be out there enjoying ourselves. We had a healthy lead at the top of the table, so we shouldn't have felt any real pressure. Big Jock asked us to go out and enjoy ourselves. By the time we reached the pitch for the start of the second half, we were really lifted.'

Within minutes, the great Davie Cooper had shot Rangers into the lead, and shortly afterwards Johnstone scored one of the best goals of his career. 'I headed the ball over Willie McVie, sprinted past him and then chipped the ball over Rennie. It wasn't so much the finish that I remember, even though it was sheer class, as you would expect,' he joked, 'but the fact that I sprinted past everybody!'

Five minutes later, Rangers added another to take the scoreline to 5–2. 'I netted my hat-trick,' claimed Derek. Not according to the records, however, which showed the last to be an own goal 'credited' to the unfortunate McVie, but then again Johnstone is a typical striker – claiming every goal he can!

In May, Rangers celebrated another Treble, and it capped a fine year for Derek Johnstone who was voted Scottish Football Writers' Associations' Player of the Year. When he hung up his boots to take up the microphone in 1986, there was at least one club glad to see the back of him – Motherwell!

AT THAT TIME

Troubles continued in Northern Ireland as three soldiers were killed on patrol when a land mine blew up their Land Rover.

For smokers, 20 Embassy Regal cigarettes cost 39p.

Motor enthusiasts could buy a 1.6l Colt Celeste for just under £2,300.

The price of a bottle of whisky was around £3.45.

On television, the popular shows included *When the Boat Comes In* and *The Six Million Dollar Man*.

In sport, Rag Trade won the Grand National at Aintree.

Sixteen-year-old Derek Johnstone scores against
Celtic in the 1970 League Cup final.

ALLY McCOIST

The charismatic Ally McCoist took a rather circuitous route to Rangers before accepting terms from manager John Greig in 1983, completing a £185,000 transfer from Sunderland. Having turned Greig down two years earlier while at St Johnstone, many considered that the likeable lad from East Kilbride had given up any chance of playing for the side he supported as a youngster. However, Greig's persistence was justified as the striker went on to become one of the finest players to wear the Light Blue of Rangers.

More the penalty box player than the typical target man, McCoist was lethal in and around the goalmouth and goals flowed, particularly in the Souness and Smith eras, as Rangers asserted their dominance over Scottish football. Despite fierce competition for the number 9 jersey from a number of quality strikers through the period, he fought off successive challenges to retain his position.

In 14 years at the club, serving under four Rangers managers, 'Super Ally', as the fans called him, broke just about every scoring record for the club. Recognition of his goal-scoring exploits extended far beyond Rangers, however, and he won the Golden Boot as top European goal scorer in consecutive seasons in 1993 and 1994. He was also voted Player of the Year by both the Scottish Football Writers' Association and by fellow players.

His goals helped Rangers to the 'Nine-in-a-Row' triumph and he was at the heart of most of Rangers' successes through the late '80s and '90s. He helped the club to ten Championships through the period, one Scottish Cup and nine League Cup triumphs. However, he is most famed for his goals and in over 580 first-class games he scored a remarkable 355 goals. His success extended beyond Rangers, with his performances taking him to 61 caps for Scotland – a club record he shares with former Ibrox teammate, Richard Gough.

When McCoist left Ibrox in 1998, he joined Kilmarnock, where he played in the Premier League for three seasons before finally hanging up his boots to pursue his blossoming television career. His talents were also extended to the cinema with a first movie appearance in 2001 alongside legendary film star Robert Duvall in a film about, naturally, football.

EUROPEAN CUP — FIRST ROUND, SECOND LEG
RANGERS 2 (Falco, McCoist) DYNAMO KIEV 0
Attendance: 44,500
Ibrox Stadium, Glasgow — 30 September 1987

RANGERS: Woods; Nicholl, Phillips, McGregor, Souness,
Butcher, Francis, Falco, McCoist, Durrant and Cohen.
DYNAMO KIEV: Chanov; Bessonov, Baltaca, Kuznetsov Yevseyev,
Ratz, Yakovenko, Mikhailichenko, Yaremchuk, Belanov and Blokhin.

Every follower of Rangers during the period 1983 to 1998 when Ally McCoist carved his name in Ibrox folklore will carry their own memory of the striker's indelible mark on the club. For many, the McCoist grin as he reeled away with the ball lodged firmly in the back of the net is a perpetual image. Goals, goals, goals, invariably followed by a cascade of silverware in one of the most sparkling periods in Rangers' history. He was at the centre of just about every match of any real significance during these glorious 15 years, often providing the lethal touch in front of goal. Quite simply, his contribution to Rangers during this period is immeasurable. How, therefore, could he single out any one match above all others?

'I'll go for the League Cup final of 1984, when I scored a hat-trick against Celtic,' he said. 'No, I'll change it! I'll pick the Dynamo Kiev game. That was more memorable.' It was typical McCoist — as evasive in his answers as he had been to countless defenders who tried unsuccessfully to tie him down throughout his career. It is little wonder he scored so many goals.

Although he won 20 major honours in his career, it is perhaps understandable that the Kiev match carried such significance for McCoist. The year was 1987, just over a year into Graeme Souness' Ibrox revolution, and Rangers had returned to the European Cup for the first time in nine seasons. The Light Blues were not given much hope when the draw paired them with the Soviet champions. Dynamo Kiev, after all, had a good European pedigree, while Rangers boss Graeme Souness' side had promise and optimism, but little else to suggest that an upset was on the cards.

McCoist recalled, 'We knew that they had a good record in Europe and had some really quality players, including Kuznetsov and Mikhailichenko [who later became his teammate at Ibrox]. We played the first leg in Kiev in front of 100,000 and did well to hold them to a 1–0 victory with their goal coming from "Chenks" [Mikhailichenko]. On the face of it, we looked to have a great chance of going through, but we knew that they were a great side. We certainly wouldn't underestimate them.'

The match captured the imagination of the Scottish public and a capacity crowd of just under 45,000 packed inside Ibrox for the return leg a fortnight later. 'We knew that we would really have to work hard to get anything from the game, but I remember that the crowd also played a major part that night. Souness had called for them to be vocal before it and I've never heard noise like it inside Ibrox.

'There was a tremendous atmosphere in the ground and enormous tension in the game, but we got a lucky break when their keeper gifted us the opening goal. He completely fumbled his throw-out, hitting Kuznetsov, and the ball landed at my feet. I turned it towards Mark Falco who had the easiest of tasks in turning it into the empty net.' The scores were level on aggregate.

Ibrox erupted as the fans sensed that this could well be Rangers' night, but there was even more joy in store for McCoist. Trevor Francis fired over a cross that was turned towards the striker by Falco. 'As the ball came over, I rose gracefully, picked my spot and headed the ball firmly goalwards! Well, actually, it glanced off my head. I tried to place it in one corner and it went into the other! It completely fooled the keeper and the noise when the ball hit the net was incredible.'

Rangers were ahead with just over 20 minutes to go. It was the longest 20 minutes in living memory as the Soviets pressed in desperation to save the tie. Minutes seemed like hours as the game crept towards the final whistle. When it finally sounded there can hardly ever have been such an explosion of joy inside the stadium. 'It was a huge relief to hear the whistle and a great feeling to win the game,' said McCoist.

No sooner had the interview with McCoist ended when the telephone rang. It was a mutual acquaintance. 'I've just spoken to Ally,' he said. It's about his match to remember. He wants to change it to the 1973

Centenary Cup final when Tom Forsyth scored the winner.' It was, apparently, his first Old Firm game. McCoist would have been about 11 years of age at the time, and clearly the match had a big impact on him, but there was no way back. Ironically, despite playing almost 600 games for Rangers, he had decided that his most memorable game was one that he hadn't even played in! Then again, that's Ally. Rangers were always more important to him than McCoist. It's just that it seemed they were virtually one and the same for a long time!

AT THAT TIME

While Rangers celebrated victory over Dynamo Kiev, Celtic swooped to sign Frank McAvennie from West Ham. A week later the Ibrox side signed Richard Gough.

The news headlines were dominated by reports of a siege at Peterhead Prison, Aberdeen.

On television, Michael Barrymore presented the popular *Strike It Lucky* while *Blackadder The Third* continued the popular series with Rowan Atkinson.

For drinkers, a can of lager cost 41p and a bottle of whisky was £7.29.

Ally McCoist in typical celebratory mood.

ROBERT RUSSELL

The Rangers side that swept to the Treble in 1978 was perhaps the fittest in the League, but there was much more to Jock Wallace's side than simple athleticism. It was a team that abounded with skill and Robert Russell was one of the shining lights, adding culture to the work-rate and power provided by the unit. Russell was signed from Shettleston Juniors and immediately graduated to the first team at just 20 years of age, holding his place in a midfield that included Alex MacDonald, Tommy McLean and Gordon Smith.

His game revolved around excellent vision and passing ability, but he also scored some important goals, most notably in the 1981 Cup final and the famous away victory over PSV Eindhoven in 1978. Russell left Ibrox in 1987 as Graeme Souness shook up the side, but he moved on to Motherwell where he continued to show the skills that had brought him international recognition.

However, just as frequent injury prevented him from making a full Scotland appearance, it also proved debilitating for the remainder of his footballing career. When he finally hung up his boots, he turned to part-time coaching and currently assists Rangers in the development of some promising youngsters.

In his ten years at Rangers, he played over 370 first-class games and won a League Championship medal, three Scottish Cups and four League Cups

SCOTTISH CUP FINAL (REPLAY)
RANGERS 4 (Cooper, Russell, MacDonald 2) DUNDEE UNITED 1 (Dodds)
Attendance: 43,099
Hampden Park, Glasgow — 12 May 1981

RANGERS: Stewart; Jardine, Dawson, Stevens, Forsyth, Bett, Cooper, Russell, Johnstone, Redford and MacDonald.
DUNDEE UNITED: McAlpine; Holt, Kopel, Phillip (Stark), Hegarty, Narey, Bannon, Milne, Kirkwood, Sturrock and Dodds.

When midfield star of the late '70s and early '80s, Robert Russell, returned to the Ibrox payroll in 1997 to assist in coaching some of the young Ibrox starlets, after a gap of 11 years, his first day proved quite emotional. As he glanced into the home dressing-room that held so many happy memories for him, he was quite unprepared for his impromptu meeting with Brian Laudrup. 'Hello Robert, I can remember seeing your goal against PSV Eindhoven. It was great football,' enthused the Dane. Russell immediately suspected a wind-up, because just about everyone wants to talk about 'that goal', but 'Lauders'' interest was genuine. 'We had a chat about the game and that match,' recalled Robert, 'but I was amazed that Laudrup had shown such interest.

'It was obviously an important moment for me when I scored the winner in that European Cup tie back in 1978, but it has been well covered over the years. However, for all that the Eindhoven game meant to me, there was another match that sticks out in my memory – the replay of the 1981 Scottish Cup final against Dundee United,' he said.

'The first match was drawn 0–0, although we had a late chance to win with a penalty after I had cut into the area and was hauled down. Ian Redford hit it tamely and McAlpine had no trouble in making the save. When we got back to the dressing-room John Greig, who was manager at the time, gave me a bit of a bawling for not shooting, but his anger was probably more out of frustration than anything.

'We returned to Hampden for the replay three days later, only this time Davie Cooper, Derek Johnstone and John MacDonald all returned to the side. With no disrespect to the players who went out, we felt that the freshness of these three would make a difference,' recalled Russell.

In fact the changes proved to be the significant factor in the tie as Rangers went on to win 4–1 with Cooper and MacDonald grabbing three of the goals between them. Russell notched the other.

'When the game started we had a good feeling about it and the tempo was noticeably faster than the first match. To some extent we felt that we had something to prove after the first game, which was really a bit of a let-down.

'The big Rangers crowd roared us on and we got the perfect start when "Coop" got the opener after only ten minutes. He then cut the ball back to me to get the second and also set up the third for John MacDonald. United did pull one back through Davie Dodds, but we went in at the break with a comfortable 3–1 lead.

'After the interval "Coop" really turned it on and, with less than 15 minutes to go, MacDonald slipped the ball through McAlpine's legs for the fourth. I can remember him running with his arms up in the air then turning round to see where the players were! He didn't get the celebrations he expected because we knew by then the game was all wrapped up, so nobody went to congratulate him,' laughed Robert.

'Dundee United didn't really offer anything in the game and their main danger man, Paul Sturrock, was well covered by big Tam Forsyth. In fact I think he was terrified of Forsyth. Tam used to growl at him and that was enough to sort him out! Tam was the bodyguard in the team, which helped the ball players.

'After the game we came back to Ibrox for the celebrations and we were joined by our families, including my father who used to go to all of the games.'

The match is often referred to as 'the Cooper Final' and there is no doubt that the late, legendary figure played a vital part in the success, but those who witnessed that memorable tie will testify that Russell, too, was an enormous influence.

Were it not for the recurring knee injuries that would eventually end his career he would undoubtedly have earned a sackload of caps. Fate conspired to force his withdrawal from several Scotland squads, but while his career was unfulfilled at international level, he did enough at Ibrox to earn the respect and adoration of thousands.

Today he has the memories of that career and the great goals. In case he should ever forget, there are always the likes of Brian Laudrup to remind him!

AT THAT TIME

Violence flared in Northern Ireland as the death of a second IRA hunger striker was announced. Meanwhile, the trial of the 'Yorkshire Ripper', Peter Sutcliffe, continued at the Old Bailey.

At Linwood, there was despair as 4,800 people prepared for the shutdown of the car factory.

On television Lena Zavaroni continued her short series of variety shows on BBC.

In England, Manchester City and Tottenham Hotspur prepared to face each other again in the English FA Cup final replay.

England lost 1–0 to Brazil at Wembley, through a goal from Zico.

Davie Cooper, the hero of the 1981
Scottish Cup final replay.

TERRY BUTCHER

Before Graeme Souness fired the Ibrox revolution in 1986 it would have been virtually unthinkable for the captain of England to join Rangers. Not that the Ibrox club was in any way inferior to sides south of the border, but the Scottish game had become well accustomed to the drain of its talent southwards, with little movement in the other direction. Souness almost single-handedly challenged the status quo and lured Terry Butcher to Rangers in the face of stern competition from the likes of Manchester United. It was a remarkable coup. Not only was Butcher the England skipper, but he was recognised to be one of the best central defenders in the game. Moreover, Rangers signalled their intent with a transfer fee of £725,000, smashing the Scottish record.

At 6 ft 4 in., Butcher was an imposing figure in the Rangers defence and Souness built his team around him in the early years. The Englishman responded with dedication and commitment to a club he quickly developed a strong affection for. He also became a big favourite with the Light Blue legions. Always a winner, his drive helped take Rangers to the Championship in that first season and, had it not been for the broken leg he sustained in the next, many consider that the Ibrox side would have regained the title. However, when he returned to the side, Rangers quickly got back on the trail, winning what was to turn out to be the first of the nine successive Championships they won through the late '80s and early '90s.

His Rangers career ended after a post-match disagreement with Graeme Souness, which both player and manager later regretted, but it brought the curtain down on a great spell for Butcher. He left for Coventry City in a deal worth £500,000 and had a dalliance with the Midlands club as manager. He also had an unsuccessful spell at Sunderland. However, despite the disappointments of his managerial career, he could not detach himself from the game completely and is now assistant manager to Eric Black at Motherwell.

Always a popular character with the Rangers support, he played almost 180 games, winning three League Championships, and two League Cups. One of the great England captains, he played 77 times for his country.

SCOTTISH PREMIER LEAGUE CHAMPIONSHIP
ABERDEEN 1 (Irvine) RANGERS 1 (Butcher)
Attendance: 22,568
Pittodrie Stadium, Aberdeen — 2 May 1987

ABERDEEN: Leighton; McKimmie, W. Miller, McLeish, Robertson;
Gray, Simpson, Irvine, Bett; Hewitt and J. Miller.
RANGERS: Woods; Nicholl, Roberts, Butcher, Munro; McPherson,
Souness, Durrant, Cooper; Fleck and McCoist.

G eorge Young, Jock Shaw, Bobby Shearer, John Greig were Rangers captains cut from the same mould. Resilient characters to a man, they were the embodiment of the Ibrox spirit, driving the team forward with the shake of a fist when needed, inspiring in their own play as they led from the front. If ever a team needed a touch of that fearless determination, it was the subdued side that Graeme Souness inherited in the summer of 1986.

Souness had not even taken his place in the manager's office when he made the initial approaches to sign Terry Butcher who was on World Cup duty with England in Mexico. Souness knew what he would be getting. As a Liverpool player, he had faced the big Ipswich defender several times in club matches, quite apart from their annual confrontation in Scotland v England clashes.

Butcher was a giant in every sense of the word. He was an intimidating character, although his physical stature belied a deft touch on the ball and a left foot that could fire passes deep into the opponents' half with deadly accuracy. When he agreed to join Rangers in August 1986, there was some scepticism that the deal would not have materialised if the Ibrox side had not put a huge contract on the table. Some even called Butcher and those who followed, mercenaries, unlikely to understand the meaning of Rangers let alone 'play for the jersey'. How wrong could they have been?

The Rangers fans immediately took to the player who quickly became the heart of Souness' new side. They were impressed by his strength and that indomitable ingredient of character that former boss Jock Wallace considered so vital to Rangers players. For his part, Butcher quickly dispelled any notion that he could not play for the jersey by showing as keen a determination and will to win as any of the great captains before him.

In his first season, he rallied the side from a disappointing start to a 19-game undefeated run in the closing stages, projecting them to the front in the Championship. 'We never really believed that we would win the League in our first year,' he admitted. 'We had so many new players and had to get used to a different style of football. We did win the Skol Cup earlier in the year, which was very satisfying, but to get the chance of taking the title was a dream.'

By May, Rangers had driven relentlessly to reach pole position in the title race, needing a victory at Aberdeen to secure the Championship in Souness' first season. The Light Blues realised that a draw might be enough, but that would depend on Celtic not taking full points from their game. Butcher recalled, 'I wasn't nervous going into the game, but things didn't work out for us at the start when Graeme Souness was sent off. We went in at the break level, but midway through the second half we got a free kick over on the left. I could see a look in Davie Cooper's eyes and I just knew where he would deliver the ball. I moved into the box and met the ball cleanly to send it past Jim Leighton and into the net.

'Aberdeen equalised from a free kick with ten minutes to go and from then on we had our backs to the wall. As the game drew to a close we heard the fans cheer and then knew that Celtic hadn't got the victory they needed. We knew that we had won the Championship.

'After the referee blew the final whistle it was pandemonium, but a great experience as the fans rallied round us. I was carried sky-high. When we got into the dressing-room I just jumped into the bath and sat there with a beer. I was on a high. After we left Pittodrie, Chris Woods, Graham Roberts and I stopped off at Roller Rocks nightclub in Stirling where we had a champagne party to ourselves. It was a long night, but a memorable one. A real match to remember.'

It was a wonderful start to Butcher's Ibrox career and of immense importance to Rangers. Souness had paved the way for a new dawn in Rangers' history – a period of untold domination. For Butcher it was the confirmation of his ascendancy to that elite group of great Rangers captains.

AT THAT TIME

The headlines were dominated by the Zeebrugge Ferry Disaster probe.

On television, *Wogan* had Lulu and Ernie Wise as guests, while *Cheers* was popular on Channel 4.

In snooker, Steve Davis took the World Professional title.

In football, Dundee United prepared to meet Gothenburg in the UEFA Cup final.

Nigel Mansell continued his dominance on the track, winning the San Marino Formula One Grand Prix.

Terry Butcher in typical pose alongside Alex McLeish
and Brian Grant of Aberdeen in a League fixture
against the Dons.

JOHN BROWN

Fans have always had a special bond with the player who 'plays for the jersey'. The self-same devotion that elevates players to idol status is, however, often unmatched by the skills that distinguish the true 'great'. Show me a dozen players that have blossomed as true Rangers men and I'll show you but a precious few whose contribution to the club extends much further that the enthusiasm of a devotee.

There are notable exceptions, however, and there can rarely be a force more potent in a team than the player who allies great skill and awareness with true allegiance to the club. In that respect, if there was ever to be the archetypal 'Rangers man' who combined devotion with ability it has got to be John Brown.

Signed almost exactly ten years ago from Dundee by Graeme Souness for the paltry fee of £350,000, Brown represented one of the finest pieces of business conducted by the former Rangers boss. At a period when versatility was the prerequisite of the modern footballer, the likeable lad from Hamilton readily slotted into various defensive and midfield roles. Whether he was seen as a pool player at the time of his acquisition is unclear, but Brown quickly established himself in the side, settling with ease alongside players with much more expensive price tags.

He eventually went on to play almost 300 games for the side and scored around 20 goals in a career that produced seven Championships, three Scottish Cup and three League Cup medals. Nowadays he is an important part of the Ibrox backroom team, acting alongside John McGregor as reserve team coach.

EUROPEAN CUP – CHAMPIONS LEAGUE (GROUP PHASE)
MARSEILLES 1 (Sauzee) RANGERS 1 (Durrant)
The Velodrome, Marseilles – 7 April 1993

MARSEILLES: Barthez; Angloma, di Meco, Boli, Sauzee, Desailly,
Eydelie, Boksic, Voller, Pele and Deschamps.
RANGERS: Goram; McCall, Robertson (Murray), Gough, McPherson,
Brown, Steven, Ferguson, McCoist, Durrant and Huistra (McSwegan).

For all the honours that John Brown won as a Rangers player, the disappointment of his failure to add a European Cup winner's medal cuts deep. It was a case of so close, yet so far. In season 1992–93 he came within 90 minutes of a place in the continent's showcase European Cup final, after a courageous run through the qualifying stages. It all came to an end in a disappointing evening at Ibrox as Rangers struggled to a 0–0 draw with CSKA Moscow, while French champions Marseilles gained the victory they needed in Bruges to take them through to a final against AC Milan. For many, however, Rangers' hopes ended in Marseilles two weeks earlier when the Light Blues failed to get the win in France that would have taken them through to the final.

Brown recalled, 'I have a lot of great memories of my career, but if there was one big disappointment it was that April night in Marseilles back in 1993. We had enjoyed a great campaign, during which we had seen off the champions of England, Leeds United, in what was dubbed the "Battle of Britain". That in itself was a match to remember, but we went on from there in the Champions League set-up, to contest the group with the best side in France – Marseilles.

'We had come back from the death in the first match at Ibrox to earn a 2–2 draw, and subsequent victories over Bruges and CSKA Moscow put us virtually in a semi-final position with the French for the return. It was clear cut – if they won, they went through. If we won, we would be in our first ever European Cup final.

'We went into the game with confidence from our domestic form and our European run – we were unbeaten in our eight matches in Europe leading up to the game. I can remember the noise inside the Velodrome Stadium when we came out. It was a real carnival atmosphere and we felt good.

'We played a back four of McPherson, Gough, myself and Robertson.

In the centre of the defence, "Goughie" and I adopted a zonal-marking system, covering areas rather than going for man-marking on their strike pairing of Rudi Voller and Alen Boksic. The system was working well and we felt that we were comfortable until they shocked us with a goal in the first half. It was a setback but we knew we could get back in the game.

'Our persistence paid off in the second half when Ian Durrant scored a wonder goal, and we knew we were just a flash away from going through – or going out. They had chances, but McCoist and McSwegan also had opportunities to snatch the vital goal. The final whistle went with the score at 1–1 and it was all down to the final sectional games. We would have to beat CSKA again and hope that Bruges did us a favour. I knew it wouldn't happen and, as I left the field in Marseilles, I realised our chance had gone. I was gutted and it was a very long journey back for all of us. It was the worst trip back that I can remember, in fact, although the press and our fans later hailed the result a great success. We arrived back in Glasgow, tired and despondent, in the early hours, but the reception from a large contingent of the Bears who greeted us lifted us all.

'Next morning, I chatted about the trip with my wife who had joined a few of the other girls on a different flight and returned separately. A little bit of humour helped break the disappointment. Apparently, as they arrived in Glasgow, the mother of one of the players noted that the flight back had taken nearly three and a quarter hours, compared to the two and a half hours on the way out. She reckoned that, since they had flown out in daylight but had come back at night, the pilot probably wouldn't have seen where he was going so clearly on the return!'

She was serious and the story brought the first smile to Bomber's face after the trauma of Marseilles. When he looks back he will realise that he was part of one of the greatest teams to wear the blue jersey and without his determination in innumerable games that season it's doubtful whether the team would have enjoyed the same level of success and got as far as they did in the European Cup that year.

While Marseilles eventually won the Cup, beating Milan in the final 1–0, the French side and their president, Bernard Tapie, were later discredited and had the trophy stripped from them. While there were suggestions of malpractice in earlier ties, Brown was quite forthright and honest. 'They were a better side than us and deserved to go through.'

Perhaps, but it was still a wonderful performance from Rangers, built on a strength of character epitomised by John Brown.

AT THAT TIME

The headlines were dominated by the tragic death of the baby daughter of former Rangers star Derek Ferguson.

A new series of *The Beechgrove Garden* kept those with green fingers entertained on BBC, with *The Bill* and *The Crystal Maze* other popular options for viewers.

In entertainment, *Blue Peter* star John Leslie dumped Catherine Zeta Jones because it was alleged that she wanted to get married too quickly.

In golf, Bernhard Langer went on to win the US Masters golf tournament.

John Brown in typical action for Rangers.

PETER McCLOY

Name any of the successful sides from the '70s or early '80s and it will inevitably begin with the name of goalkeeper Peter McCloy. Signed from Motherwell in 1970 by Willie Waddell in a swap deal that took Bobby Watson and Brian Heron to Fir Park, the imposing figure of McCloy provided a solid base to the rebuilding process the club so desperately needed at that time.

At 6 ft 4 in., he was a towering figure in the Rangers goal and, in a reference to the hometown where he still resides, he was dubbed the 'Girvan Lighthouse'. In a career that spanned 16 seasons, McCloy faced competition from a number of goalkeepers, but eventually won through to hold his place. He shared in much of the success that the club enjoyed through the '70s, including the famous European Cup Winners' Cup win in 1972 and the Treble successes of 1976 and 1978.

By this time he hung up his boots to turn to coaching he had played over 530 games with Rangers and registered over 210 shoot-outs. He won a championship medal, four Scottish Cups and four League Cups in a career which also brought four caps for Scotland.

EUROPEAN CUP WINNERS' CUP FINAL
RANGERS 3 (Stein, Johnston 2) MOSCOW DYNAMO 2 (Eschtrekov, Makovikov)
Attendance: 45,000
Nou Camp Stadium, Barcelona — 24 May 1972

RANGERS: McCloy, Jardine, Mathieson, Greig, D. Johnstone,
Smith, McLean, Conn, Stein, MacDonald and W. Johnston.
MOSCOW DYNAMO: Pilgui, Basalev, Dolmatov, Zykov, Dobbonosov (Gerschkovitch),
Zhukov, Baidatchini, Jakubik (Eschtrekov), Sabo, Makovikov and Evryuzhikbin.

uropean football figured prominently in Peter McCloy's career with
Rangers right from the outset. His acquisition from Motherwell
was prompted in some way by the club's failure in Europe. Under
Davie White, Rangers crashed (1–3) to Polish side Gornik Zabre on a cold
November night at Ibrox in 1969. White was promptly dismissed and new
boss, Willie Waddell, moved quickly to reconstruct the side. McCloy was
his first major signing and soon became a firmly established member of the
side. Within 30 months, Waddell turned the side around in a quite
remarkable manner by taking the Light Blues to the European Cup
Winners' Cup final. Were it not for Rangers' failure against Gornik, the
'Gers keeper might never have ended up at Ibrox, but, ironically, the very
competition that was the catalyst for his move provided the setting for the
highlight of his career – in an historic night in Barcelona in 1972.

Unsurprisingly, McCloy remembers the occasion with fervour. 'I played
a tremendous number of games for Rangers and many are no more than
vague images, but the Barcelona trip will always remain fresh in my mind.
We travelled to Spain with wives and girlfriends and Willie Waddell
booked the squad into a remote hotel in the mountains. That allowed us to
prepare for the game in peace, but I understand the Russians were booked
into one of the tourist hotels on the front. That couldn't have been ideal for
them with all of the holidaymakers around.'

If the accommodation was strange for the Russians, Rangers had quite
different circumstances to contend with. They went into the match as firm
favourites, which was an odd experience for the players after the earlier
rounds. McCloy recalls, 'In the early stages of the competition we were
probably regarded as no-hopers, but after defeating the likes of Sporting
Lisbon and Bayern Munich we earned a lot of respect. So, going into the
final, many reckoned we were favourites to take the Cup.

'As we went about our preparations we knew that it was a huge game for
the club, but, strangely, it didn't really hit home until we took the bus to the
Nou Camp Stadium. We had seen the ground the day before, but as we
approached the stadium with only a couple of hours to kick-off we were
astonished by the huge Rangers support. It just seemed like a home game.
The bus went silent and we realised then just how important this game was
to the fans. We were truly taken aback by the response.

'That was, in fact, the core of Waddell's pre-match talk with us. I
remember him saying, "Look how much it means to these people."

'As we took to the field we were in a positive frame of mind, which was
no surprise with something like about nine internationalists in the side. My

parents were in the ground and I recall waving to them, but we were all focused on the job ahead. The events of the match have been well documented, and many people remember my huge hoist upfield, which led to the third goal. We used to come under some criticism for playing the long ball, but we had speedy forwards who could capitalise. An early goal from Colin Stein, then a second from Willie Johnston before half-time put us into a comfortable position. Early in the second half I hoisted a kick deep into their half and "Bud" was just caught offside. He got the next one, however, after it broke from Colin Stein's header and he rounded the keeper to put us 3–0 up.

'Our biggest danger at that stage was getting carried away with the whole occasion and we did lose a bit of concentration to let them score two late goals, but overall we had defended well. A photographer behind the goal kept me in touch with the time as we saw out the last few nervous moments. After the final whistle we were elated with the win, but disappointed that we could not show the fans the trophy. It was then back to the hotel and the wives joined up with us for the celebrations, which went on long and hard into the evening.

'Many years on I still look at my jersey and medal, although they are currently on display at the SFA museum. I hope they will go on display at Ibrox sometime. On my fiftieth birthday a few years ago, my wife arranged for a wooden name sign for the house. It is called "Nou Camp".'

That famous stadium in Barcelona will always hold a special place in the heart of Peter McCloy. The Cup Winners' Cup, which provided much sadness to many Rangers players in the past, had been the catalyst for the keeper's move to Ibrox. It was fitting that three years on he should revel in the glory of that famous win in Barcelona – a victory that signalled the rebirth of Rangers.

AT THAT TIME

The news was dominated by the crowd disturbances that followed Rangers' win and reports of a possible ban facing the Ibrox club.

Before the match, travel agents were offering flights to Barcelona on a 24-hour return trip for £33.50.

Other news focused on the *Queen Elizabeth II* liner, which was subject to a bomb scare and a demand for ransom money.

On television, Arthur Negas created interest in antiques with *Going for a Song*.

In the cinema, the main features were *Dirty Harry* and *The French Connection*.

Colin Stein turns away in celebration after opening the
scoring for Rangers in Barcelona, 1972.

DAVID ROBERTSON

Few players contributed more to the 'Nine-in-a-Row' campaign than former Rangers defender David Robertson. In the six seasons he enjoyed at Ibrox he was never once on a losing Championship side, and added three Scottish Cup and three League Cup medals to his collection of honours. His gutsy performances characterised a Rangers side with an inbuilt determination to complete that historic sequence of titles.

Signed from Aberdeen in 1991 for a fee of £970,000, his career was slow in progressing at Ibrox in the early stages, as he failed to find the form that he had shown at Pittodrie. However, when he settled into Ibrox, and Glasgow, he quickly became a solid part of the Walter Smith side that was to dominate through the '90s.

An attacking full-back, he formed a great understanding with Brian Laudrup in as formidable a left-flank partnership as any seen at Rangers. His strength and strong running was ideally suited to the hard-working side that Smith had assembled. The highlights of his career included Rangers' magnificent Champions League run in 1993, the Treble success that same season and, ultimately, the 'Nine-in-a-Row' conquest.

In his seven seasons at Ibrox he played in over 250 games and scored 19 goals. He also won three caps for Scotland.

SCOTTISH CUP FINAL
RANGERS 2 (Murray, Hateley) ABERDEEN 1 (Richardson)
Attendance: 50,175
Celtic Park, Glasgow — 29 May 1993

RANGERS: Goram; McCall, Robertson, Gough, McPherson, Brown, Murray, Ferguson, Durrant, Hateley and Huistra (Pressley).
ABERDEEN: Snelders; McKimmie, Wright (Smith), Grant, Irvine, McLeish, Richardson, Mason, Booth, Shearer (Jess) and Paatelainen.

T here were many people unhappy to see the departure of David Robertson to Leeds United in 1997, not least the player himself. A feeling of rejection and a breakdown in contract negotiations convinced the full-back that his future lay elsewhere, but the transition was not an easy one. The situation was compounded by a knee injury that prevented his career at Elland Road from ever seriously getting off the ground and ultimately cut it prematurely short. For Robertson, there would be good cause to rue the day he left Rangers, but he is reflective. 'I enjoy life in the south,' said 'Robbo', 'but there are many times when I miss Ibrox and Glasgow. Although I was born and bred in Aberdeen, most of my friends live in the city and I regard Glasgow as my home now.'

It was a home that provided many happy memories both on and off the field. On the personal front he settled into married life with young kids in tow. On the field he was part of one of the most successful periods in the club's history – a spell when it seemed that just about every game carried immense importance with silverware at stake. However, there was one match that stood above all others in Robertson's mind as 'typifying the resilience and character of one of the best sides we had during my spell,' he said. 'The Scottish Cup final of season 1992–93 was the culmination of possibly one of the best years in the club's history. We had already won the League and League Cup by the time the match came around and this was the chance for the Treble.

'The season was a long, but memorable one. During the campaign we had our famous run in the Champions League when we remained undefeated in ten games, although we lost out narrowly in our section to Marseilles.' It was so close yet so far in Europe, but Rangers surged through the Championship and had the League Cup in the Ibrox trophy room by the time they went to Celtic Park for the final, as Hampden was under reconstruction. Robertson recalled, 'By the time we got to the final against Aberdeen, we had played over 60 games that season and I had played in 57 of them.

'The lead-up to the game was reasonably normal for us. We travelled to Turnberry and stayed down there before travelling back to Glasgow for the match preparations. In the city we prepared much as we would for a normal game, staying overnight at a Glasgow hotel. The team wasn't announced until the day of the match, although I was expecting to be included. In the morning we read the newspapers and then focused on the fact that we were on the verge of a little bit of history with the Treble up for grabs. We were fired up for it, but knew that the game would not be easy.

'We were confident and determined when we got to Celtic Park. From the start of the game we took the initiative and first-half goals from Mark Hateley and Neil Murray seemed to set us well on our way. We were comfortable until Richardson pulled one back for the Dons in the closing stages. By this time tiredness was beginning to set in as the long season began to take its toll, and in the last 20 minutes we had to defend frantically. We were clearing the ball anywhere at the death and I remember one clearance late on from John Brown when he hooked the ball away from the line.

'The fighting spirit and determination to work for each other was characteristic of that side and there was a real feeling of being a unit. I was marking Paul Mason, who was a friend in my Aberdeen days. We still keep in touch, but that day I had him under control – well, for 80 minutes anyway!

'When the whistle went there was a sense of relief that we had completed a memorable season in the best possible way. My family was there to celebrate the victory back at Ibrox and we made the most of it. The next season was a total contrast when we lost in the final to Dundee United when going for back-to-back Trebles. But no one could take the achievement of 1992–93 away from us.'

David Robertson has moved on now and the disappointment of his departure from Ibrox has long since faded. What remains instead is an intimate love for the club, developed during one of the finest spells in the club's history. It was more than a moment in time. It was six years of sustained success.

AT THAT TIME

Media attention focused on the Royal Family, with the press accusing both Prince Charles and Princess Diana of putting on a show of happiness as speculation mounted about their marriage.

On television, Freddie Starr delivered a one-hour special, while Paul Young continued his popular fishing programme, *Hooked on Scotland*.

In football, Scottish clubs voted for a change to the set-up, with four leagues planned for the next season.

Elsewhere, Marseilles celebrated after their victory over AC Milan in the European Cup final with Basile Boli scoring the only goal.

A smiling Davie Robertson in training.

ROBERT PRYTZ

With the pressure building on manager John Greig to bring the Championship to Ibrox in the face of stern competition from Celtic and 'New Firm' rivals Aberdeen and Dundee United, he boosted his squad with the acquisition of Swedish internationalist Robert Prytz, followed by Craig Paterson from Hibernian. Prytz was signed from Malmo for a fee of around £100,000 and looked to be a sound piece of business. When he joined Rangers he had already earned ten caps for his country and helped his club to the European Cup final in 1979, where they narrowly lost to Nottingham Forest.

Prytz had an immediate impact on Greig's side, adding dynamism and a touch of class to Rangers. But, while he himself could not turn around the club's fortunes for Greig, he did go on to earn success during a solid Ibrox career. By the time he left Ibrox in 1985, a year before the Souness revolution, he had played 117 first-class matches and scored 20 goals. With the misfortune of representing the club during a relatively barren spell, Prytz has only one medal to show for his contribution to Rangers, a League Cup winner's medal from 1985. However, he was a popular player among the Light Blue legions and, with his home in Glasgow, he is a regular visitor to the stadium.

An enthusiast for the game, Prytz was still playing for Hamilton at the age of 41, before devoting more attention to the coaching side of the game. Among the clubs he has represented in almost 25 years of football are Gothenburg, Bayer Leverkusen and Verona.

SCOTTISH PREMIER LEAGUE CHAMPIONSHIP
ABERDEEN 1 (Strachan) RANGERS 2 (Johnstone, Prytz)
Attendance: 22,000
Pittodrie Stadium, Aberdeen – 25 September 1982

ABERDEEN: Leighton; Kennedy, McLeish, Miller, Rougvie; Strachan, Simpson, Cooper; Bell, McGhee and Black.
RANGERS: Stewart; McKinnon, Paterson, McClelland, Dawson; Russell, Bett, Prytz, Redford; Johnstone and Cooper.

With foreign players more of the norm around Ibrox nowadays, Swede Robert Prytz may be expected to have more affinity with the new breed than with the Scottish players who were once the core of the club. However, long before Jorg Albertz took to the local dialogue with quaint colloquialisms like 'nae bother', Prytz had more than ingratiated himself with the Glasgow public, immersing himself so much into the city that it now is to every intent his home. 'I can never see me returning to Sweden,' he says. Despite leaving Ibrox and heading home to Scandinavia in 1985 before journeying again to Italy and Germany, he hankered for a return to Glasgow with his city-born wife.

The little Swede has many happy memories of his playing days at Ibrox and is always welcomed whenever he returns to see a Rangers side that bears little resemblance to the one he played for. Then, he was the only player from outside the British Isles in the squad. Indeed, there were few other foreign players in the Scottish League at the time, although Scandinavians were no strangers to Rangers or several of the other top sides in the country.

However, Robert Prytz offered a lot of promise to Rangers on his arrival from Malmo. He brought experience of European and international football and, unlike many foreign players, combined grit and determination with good skills. Signed as a central or right-sided midfielder, he played his early matches for the club in his favoured position. However, after a dismal start to the Championship campaign, with two draws in the first couple of matches, manager John Greig took his side to face Aberdeen at Pittodrie, a ground that had held little success for Rangers for several years.

Prytz recalled, 'Aberdeen had a good team at that time. They had beaten us comfortably in the Scottish Cup final just before I signed and Alex Ferguson had them fired up. They had a lot of good players, including Alex McLeish and Willie Miller in the middle of their defence, with Gordon Strachan in the midfield. Up front there was Eric Black and Mark McGhee.

'When we arrived at the ground, John Greig told me I was playing on the left wing. I had played there before with Malmo, but I preferred the middle of the midfield, which was my best position. At that time, we played a 4-4-2 formation with Derek Johnstone and, generally, John MacDonald up front. On this occasion, Greig picked Ian Redford to play alongside Derek. Davie Cooper was put out on the right wing.

'We were up for the game and quickly took control. I was enjoying being involved a lot in the play on the wing. We were level at half-time, but just after the break, Derek Johnstone scored. We continued to press forward and then I got the second goal – with my head! It was my fourth goal for Rangers, but everyone was surprised that this wee tiny Swede should pop up among all these big defenders to score!

'Although Aberdeen pulled one back late in the game, we went on to win. When I got back into the dressing-room, Greigy said, "I didn't think you could head the ball." I said something about him learning about me every day, but it was a great day made all the better when I read the newspapers next day. Apparently we hadn't won at Pittodrie for about seven years.'

In fact, Rangers' last victory at the Aberdeen ground was almost eight years earlier in December 1974. Prytz' goal had helped Rangers secure their first Premier League win in Aberdeen. While it was to no avail in terms of the final destination of the title, which went to Dundee United, it was nonetheless a great experience for the Swede.

After the Pittodrie game, Prytz reverted to his traditional midfield role, but he played on the wing again that season, and scored again with his head in another game. While there was little denying his most productive role in the side was in the central midfield, ironically there was another memorable game in which he featured on the wing and scored in a stunning victory.

In 1984, under Jock Wallace, Robert Prytz was pitched in on the left wing to try to salvage Rangers' hopes of progress in the UEFA Cup against Inter Milan. After a 3–0 defeat in the first leg, there looked to be little hope for the Light Blues, but a stirring performance and a 3–1 win almost took them to a stunning reversal.

Prytz recalled, 'When Dave Mitchell got the first goal early on, the noise in the stadium was tremendous. I thought the whole place was going to lift off. If it hadn't have been for our failure to go through, I would have selected this match as my most memorable without a doubt.'

Despite winning only a solitary League Cup medal in 1985, Prytz has many fond memories of Ibrox. Sweden may be the land of his birth, but there is little doubt that Glasgow is his home and Rangers remains firmly in his heart.

AT THAT TIME

Michael Fagan was found not guilty of trespassing after being found in the Queen's bedroom at Buckingham Palace.

In the cinema, *Conan the Barbarian* made its début in Glasgow.

On television, Esther Rantzen presented *That's Life* on the BBC while Clive James took a popular look at the box on his own late-night show on ITV.

Disco lovers in Glasgow had a choice between The Ultrateque and the Savoy.

In football, Liverpool were the early leaders of the English First Division while Rangers were two points behind Celtic in Scotland.

Robert Prytz expertly scores a penalty against Valletta, in Malta.

DEREK FORBES

Bass player Derek Forbes joined Glasgow band Simple Minds in the late '70s just as they were growing away from their punk roots and reinventing themselves with a distinctive, refined sound that brought them immediate attention. Led by frontman Jim Kerr, the group went on to achieve success in both UK and America, topping the charts on both sides of the Atlantic. With a stream of albums to his credit, Forbes split with the group in 1985, then, after a spell with various other bands, including Propaganda, and session work with Kirstie McColl and others, he returned. His reunion with Kerr and the other mainstream band member Charlie Burchill took place in 1996 when he set to work on a new album.

Later, the band, with Forbes in his rightful place, went on their European Festival tour, but the remarriage of the members was short lived. In 1999 they split once again. Forbes' relationship with Burchill and Kerr has often been strained, not least because of their divergence of opinion on footballing matters, but there is a general agreement that the band is at its best with the members united and Forbes in harness.

Simple Minds recently celebrated the launch of their *Greatest Hits* album, to which Derek Forbes made an important contribution.

A fanatical Rangers fan, Forbes is a regular visitor to Ibrox and over the years he has built up a strong relationship with former Light Blues stars Ian Durrant and Ally McCoist.

SCOTTISH PREMIER LEAGUE CHAMPIONSHIP
RANGERS 5 (McCoist 2, Wilkins, Drinkell, Walters) CELTIC 1 (McAvennie)
Attendance: 44,000
Ibrox Stadium, Glasgow – 27 August 1989

RANGERS: Woods; Stevens, Brown, Gough, Wilkins, Butcher,
Drinkell, Ferguson, McCoist, Durrant (Souness) and Walters (Cooper).
CELTIC: Andrews; Morris, Rogan, Aitken, McCarthy, Grant, Stark (Miller),
McStay, McAvennie, Walker and Burns (Whyte).

P op group Simple Minds is often most closely associated with Celtic, through the lead singer Jim Kerr's much publicised affection for the club. However, bass player and former band member Derek Forbes is as enthusiastic a Rangers fan as you will find.

Despite their divergence on footballing matters, musically the band were united and at the top of the profession – with No. 1s both in the United States and Britain. Success has taken the band around the world, receiving the adulation of fans from countries far and wide. At times Glasgow must have seemed like a distant memory for the group, but while many are lured to the west coast of the States and London, this is Forbes' home and after touring he always returns home to Scotland. He regards Ibrox Stadium, where he was brought up in the faith that is Rangers, as very much part of that home.

'I remember my first game at the stadium back in the mid-'60s when we defeated Hamilton 4–0. I was amazed by the sheer size of the ground and the fans. It really was quite awesome for a youngster. That really started me off and I remember that I always seemed to leave the ground at the same time as Orjan Persson and Roger Hynd when I made my way home off along Edmiston Drive,' recalled Derek.

'My favourite player around that time was Willie "Bud" Johnston and I still have his autograph. I nearly got Willie Henderson's too, but he was in a rush and wouldn't stop.

'I also remember one of my first European matches abroad when we lost out to Borussia Munchengladbach in December 1986. We had drawn the first game at Ibrox, 1–1, and went to Germany needing a goal. I can recall Davie Cooper being hacked all over the place, but the referee took no action. Then he shocked us by sending off Stuart Munro. But the one moment from that game that really sticks in my mind was when "Coop" went to take a corner and was bitten on the backside by a police Alsatian! We never got the goal we were looking for and went out on away goals,' said Derek.

These were some of his early memories of Rangers, but he highlighted one game that will long be revered as a historic Rangers victory. 'That famous 5–1 win over Celtic back in 1989 has got to be my all-time most memorable match,' said the popster with a smile.

'While a few people were a bit uncertain of our chances going into the game, I was confident, as I always am when playing Celtic. We simply destroyed them that day and I recall Mark Walters was in great form. I can also remember singing about Ian "Julie" Andrews, the Celtic goalkeeper who had a nightmare that day and never really recovered his career afterwards.

'I hadn't been long married at that time and I remember going back completely hoarse! My wife couldn't understand why I had got so worked up about the game! That wasn't the end of it, however. I was due to leave for Germany to record with a band called Propaganda and the loss of my voice set us back a bit.'

He did eventually manage to cut the album with Propaganda and had a great career with them until 1992. After a couple of years with a Japanese band, he was to return to Simple Minds in 1996 in a reformation of the band that topped the pop world through the '80s. Derek spent seven years with the group after first joining them in 1978, and was a key element in the success that took them to international prominence, although the band did have their disagreements around the times of Old Firm games. 'They even put the Celtic crest on the drum kit, so I used to get a bit of my own back by wearing a Rangers jersey!' laughed Derek.

With Derek's return to the fold, Simple Minds discovered their old magic and celebrated with a successful new album. Future gigs in Glasgow looked certain, but Derek would have liked nothing more than to play at the stadium that holds so many happy memories. With lead singer Jim Kerr an avid Celtic fan, selection of the venue for such a concert might have been complicated, although the band did play at Ibrox in the '80s after Forbes had left. Things were much easier for Forbes in the band with a new drummer, Mel Gaynor, a staunch Rangers fan, but eventually both departed.

'I try to take in a lot of games now that I can control my diary a bit better,' said Derek, before pointing out, 'I said that my favourite player was Willie Johnston, but for a long spell I would tell Ally McCoist that it was him. That had absolutely nothing to do with the fact that the Rangers legend is a pal and was a good source of tickets! With him away now, come back Bud!'

AT THAT TIME

The headlines were dominated by a tragedy in Germany when three Italian air force jets crashed at an air show, killing at least 46 people.

In athletics, Tom McLean had a gutsy win over Sebastian Coe in the 800 metres in Berlin.

On television, *Miami Vice* was popular on the BBC, while youngsters got the chance to take part in *The Young Krypton Factor*, a quiz show with some variations on the adult version.

In golf, Sandy Lyle faded in the final round of the World Series behind Tom Watson and eventual winner Mike Reid.

In the charts, the No. 1 spot was held by Yazz and the Plastic Population with 'The Only Way is Up'.

Great Ibrox hero of the '60s and '70s, Willie Johnston.

IAN DURRANT

Reared close to Ibrox, it was a natural transition for Ian Durrant to join Rangers as an impressive schoolboy. He learned his trade under John Greig, who recognised that the youngster had sublime skills and a good attitude towards the game. When he made his début for the first team, under the management of Jock Wallace in 1984, there was a general recognition that Durrant had an immense career ahead of him.

He blossomed under Graeme Souness and, with caps at every level, it seemed that Rangers had unearthed possibly one of the greatest players ever to wear a blue jersey. A left-sided midfield player, he was every manager's dream: intelligent, cultured and direct. He was just 22, however, when he sustained an injury in an off-the-ball challenge during a match at Aberdeen. His right knee was virtually shattered and he was left with a long road to recovery. Recover he did, though, and while it is sheer conjecture as to whether he ever attained the level he would have, had he not sustained the injury, he played a vital role in Rangers' quest for 'Nine-in-a-Row'.

The pinnacle of his Rangers dream came in a match against the Light Blues' Old Firm rivals at Celtic Park, which virtually sealed the Ibrox club's triumph. Indeed, he maintains that he got the final touch in the crucial goal that was credited to Brian Laudrup. It was, regardless, a fine moment for Durrant who had made a habit of scoring important goals for Rangers. He also won back his place in the Scotland side.

By the time he left Ibrox to join Kilmarnock in 1997, he had played over 350 games for the club and scored around 50 goals. It was a career that brought him six League Championship medals, three Scottish Cups and four League Cups. Who knows what he would have attained but for his injury. It was, nevertheless, a remarkable career.

SCOTTISH PREMIER LEAGUE CHAMPIONSHIP
RANGERS 1 (Durrant) CELTIC 0
Attendance: 43,502
At Ibrox Stadium — 31 August 1986

Rangers: Woods; Nicholl, Butcher, McPherson, Munro; Fraser, Ferguson,
Durrant, McMinn, McCoist and Cooper.
Celtic: Bonner; W. McStay, Aitken, McGrigan, Whyte; P. McStay, MacLeod,
Burns, Grant; McClair and Johnston.

F ew players savoured the atmosphere of an Old Firm match more
than Ian Durrant. In 12 seasons, he played over 30 times against
Celtic, winning more than his fair share and contributing the vital
goal in some notable clashes. Indeed, he scored the opening goal in a 2–1
win over Celtic in 1986 that gave Souness the League Cup, and who could
forget his role in the goal that all but clinched the title and the 'Nine-in-
a-Row' for Rangers in 1997?

Sure, Laudrup got a touch on that occasion and then scored the
memorable goal at Tannadice that sealed the 'Nine', but for many, the
decisive strike at Celtic Park was Durrant's. It was a match to remember,
but it was not the game that Durrant savours most in a myriad of great
Rangers victories.

Instead, he vividly recalls an Old Firm encounter at Ibrox many years
earlier. The year was 1986 and Rangers were on the threshold of a
revolution that would thrust them to the top of Scottish football after years
in the wilderness. Graeme Souness didn't so much breeze into the Scottish
game that year, as hit it with the full force of a hurricane. The 19-year-old
Durrant watched big-money transfers arrive around him in a flurry of
spending, but his precocious talents were well admired by Souness, and he
held the place in the side he had earned under outgoing boss, Jock Wallace.

Souness' season got off to the worst possible start with defeat and a red
card at Easter Road. Four games into the Championship, Rangers were
behind Celtic with the first Old Firm clash looming.

Durrant recalled, 'I can remember the game was televised live, but there
was the usual big crowd at Ibrox. We knew even at that stage in the season
that we had to win, realising that victory would put us ahead of Celtic;
defeat would leave us trailing.

'I went through my usual routine. I arrived at the ground around 12 o'clock, attended to tickets and then dumped my gear in the dressing-room. I then headed up to Tiny's kitchen for lunch.'

Invariably at this time some players would have a tingle of nerves, while others anxiously watched the 'favourite' toil in the 1.30 p.m. race at Ayr. Then they would go downstairs to get the team news as the crowd filtered into Ibrox.

'When Souness read out the team, I was delighted to hear that I was in the side. I looked across the dressing-room and saw my number 10 jersey hanging on the peg. I wasn't so much nervous as determined to go out and enjoy myself. Most of the younger players were like that. It was the older ones who got a bit more uptight.

'With the minutes ticking past towards kick-off, the Gaffer [Souness] was quite quiet. He didn't say much because he didn't need to. In contrast, our captain, Terry Butcher, was firing us all up, saying things like, "Nobody beats us at Ibrox" and the like. He was a great inspiration for games like that.

'We played 4-4-2 that day and I shared the centre of the midfield with Derek Ferguson, in direct opposition to Celtic's Peter Grant and Paul McStay. Cammy Fraser took the right flank and the irrepressible Ted McMinn was on the left. McCoist and Cooper were up front.

'We quickly took the initiative from the kick-off and continued to press through the first half, but couldn't get a goal. With the scoreline blank we went inside and Souness told us to keep things going. He told us that it was only a matter of time before we got the breakthrough.

'Early into the second half, Davie Cooper saw me make a run through the Celtic defence and played one of those almost telepathic passes that only he could. He knew the runs I would make in a game and played these wonderful passes so often, splitting defences wide open. I found myself one-on-one with Packy Bonner and, as he went down a touch early, I slipped the ball past him and into the net. As I turned away in delight, Coop stood in my line with arms open ready for the celebration. The comical thing was that I totally blanked him as I ran past him towards the ecstatic fans in the enclosure, as I always did. It was one of the best "rubbers" that you could give anyone! We had a good laugh about it later.

'Late in the game I scored again, but the goal was disallowed for offside. One goal was enough, however. My whole family was there to see me, and my mum and dad came in to the Players' Lounge afterwards to join the celebrations. Only a few years earlier, as a young fan, I had sneaked into games at the Centenary Stand, but now I was a part of it all. It was hard to come to terms with it all. That evening I went out with a few of the lads for a "wee meal". We knew we had secured an important victory.'

That exquisitely worked goal was enough to give Rangers an advantage they would not lose and, by May, they were crowned Scottish Champions. It was the first of six championships for the midfielder and, had serious injury not robbed him of three good years, he would have joined Ferguson, McCoist and Gough as the only players to have played in every season of the 'Nine-in-a-Row'. These successes were born from Rangers' dominance of Celtic through the period and Durrant had more than a little influence in these contests.

'Nobody beats us at Ibrox, particularly Celtic,' Terry Butcher would say while rallying his teammates. With Durrant in the side that was generally the case!

AT THAT TIME

Sixty people were killed when a mid-air collision involving two jets took place over Los Angeles.

Actress Pat Phoenix (*Coronation Street*) and Scots entertainer Andy Stewart were both in hospital. Phoenix was fighting cancer, while Stewart was recovering from a stomach operation.

On television, Richard Attenborough's fascinating *Life on Earth* series continued on the BBC, while cycling enthusiasts enjoyed the novel Kelloggs Start City Centre Challenge which took the sport around the country's major cities.

In sport, Steve Cram won a gold medal for Britain in the 1986 Stuttgart European Athletic Championships. Meanwhile, also in Germany, Bernhard Langer won the German Open Golf Championship.

Ian Durrant in action for Rangers.

IAN FERGUSON

It is indicative of Ian Ferguson's popularity with football managers that he was bought by Graeme Souness, retained by Walter Smith and then finally included within Dick Advocaat's plans for the rehabilitation of Rangers after many of his teammates departed. A strong, wholehearted midfielder, Ferguson started his career at Clyde before joining St Mirren in 1986 for a fee of around £60,000. He quickly gained widespread recognition and a place in the Love Street history books when he scored the only goal in the Paisley side's dramatic Scottish Cup win in 1987.

Rangers tracked his progress and in 1988 Souness paid £700,000 to take him to Ibrox. Although he struggled in the early stages of his career to fulfil his price tag, his strength and shooting ability gradually won over the support.

By the time Walter Smith took over at Ibrox, the focus was firmly on the quest for 'Nine-in-a-Row' and, as an avid Rangers fan, 'Fergie' was at the forefront of the challenge. His career occasionally punctuated by injury, he did, nevertheless, play a vital role in Rangers' seemingly unending success through the early part of the '90s, and helped the club complete the sequence of titles they so desired.

When Advocaat took the reins at Rangers, he saw Ferguson as an important influence on his newly constructed side, both on and off the field. Ferguson rewarded him, playing a pivotal role as the club swept the board in the new manager's first season. In 1999, his best days behind him, Ferguson moved to Dunfermline Athletic, but he was still welcomed by the crowds whenever he returned to play at Ibrox.

Always regarded as a 'Rangers man', he ended his days at the club with a haul which included ten Championships, two Scottish Cups and five League Cups. He played over 350 games for the club, scoring about 50 goals. He also won nine caps for Scotland.

SCOTTISH PREMIER LEAGUE CHAMPIONSHIP
CELTIC 0 RANGERS 1 (Laudrup)
Attendance: 49,929
Celtic Park, Glasgow — 16 March 1997

RANGERS: Dibble; Cleland, Albertz, Gough (Miller), McLaren, Bjorklund,
Moore, Ferguson, Durrant (McCoist), Hateley and Laudrup.
CELTIC: Kerr, Annoni, McKinlay, McNamara, MacKay, Grant (Hannah),
Di Canio, McStay, Stubbs (Donnelly), O'Donnell and Cadete.

I t is hard to imagine a player who enjoyed beating Celtic more than Ian
Ferguson. Brought up within a stone's throw of Celtic Park, Ferguson
is the archetypal 'Rangers man'. He is the kind of player who always
plays for the jersey. If he was not on the field of play you would find him
in the crowd with a blue scarf wrapped around his neck. But there is much
more to Fergie's game than blue-blooded commitment.

He was plucked from St Mirren by former boss Graeme Souness, who
undoubtedly saw many of his own characteristics in the youngster: good
skills allied to a fierce will to win.

If Souness launched Fergie's career at Ibrox, it was Walter Smith who
guided him through most of his 11 years and, in return, enjoyed the
greatest benefit from the influential midfielder's play. Today Ferguson is
one of an elite trio who possess nine consecutive Championship medals.

As a youngster he had suffered the taunts that many Rangers fans
endured when Celtic embarked on their apparently never-ending
succession of titles back in the late '60s and early '70s. 'Nine-in-a-Row'
they sang and it seemed the only way to exorcise those bitter memories
would be to equal the feat, or better it. As Walter Smith's side added title
number six, then seven and eight, every Rangers fan dared to dream the
dream – none more so than Ian Ferguson. With the prize of nine successive
titles for Rangers lying within touching distance in season 1996–97, it was
no surprise that only Celtic stood between Rangers and that historic ninth
championship.

As the season moved towards a conclusion, the fixture list conspired to
provide the perfect setting. With only a few games left, Rangers were
scheduled to travel to Celtic Park for a game that many considered could
effectively decide the destination of the title. Rangers' preparations were

not ideal. Just a week before the critical League game, Celtic knocked Rangers out of the Scottish Cup (0–2), giving the Parkhead side a distinct psychological edge. How did Ferguson feel going into such a crucial game having lost out just sevens days earlier?

'Like the whole team, I was confident but very nervous as the game approached,' recalled Fergie. 'I didn't sleep very well that night (which was normal for me before an Old Firm match) and I got up at the crack of dawn, throwing open the curtains. I went for the newspapers then tried to just pace myself through to the kick-off, but I was excited. You just can't beat the feeling of going into that game! Funnily enough I always imagined that the nerves would ease as I got older, but the opposite was the case.

'A lot of the nerves came from our awareness of that defeat a week earlier, but we were well fired up. Some of the lads had taken a bit of stick after the Cup match, with some people saying that they weren't up for it. We all had something to prove after that game, so we were really focused for the match. We also knew that we had to get the victory if we wanted "the Nine".

'While we were nervous, we were also very confident. Our confidence came from knowing that we had beaten Celtic a good few more times than they had beaten us, with a number of these wins coming at Celtic Park.

'I'm not overly superstitious, but I insisted on my father being in the stand, because we rarely lost when he was there. The only other superstition I have concerns magpies. I don't like to see one before a game, and if I do, I need to spend a bit of time driving around looking for another one! Thankfully, I didn't see any that day.

'As soon as the game kicked off the nerves disappeared and I knew that we would win. From the very first tackle there was more urgency and aggression in our play than we had shown a week earlier. We battled away and I settled into my holding role. The break came just before half-time. Ian Durrant broke; with the Celtic defence at sea, he chased up the left wing, then turned the loose ball over Stewart Kerr, and goalwards. Laudrup chased in on goal and the ball was scrambled over the line. As the ball bounced into the back of the net, the noise was deafening and we went wild with delight.

'Despite losing Mark Hateley, who was sent off in the second half, we cruised out to a 1–0 victory. At the end of the match I exchanged words with Celtic's volatile winger, Paulo Di Canio, and he just lost the place. He made a big scene, but I didn't want any of that. I was conscious that if I got involved in any way it could create problems off field, so I palmed him away. The whole incident was blown out of proportion, mind you.

'Inside the dressing-room we really let our hair down because we knew that we had won the title, even though we had still to get a point in midweek from Dundee United at Tannadice to make sure. It was a big relief for everyone. It was special to me because here was a boy from the east end who was playing for Rangers among some real greats. To play alongside the likes of Butcher, Wilkins, Steven, Durrant and McCoist, as I have over the years, had been a long dream. Even now I pinch myself and reflect on these 9 Championships in 11 happy years. Despite my long service at Ibrox I never took my involvement for granted.'

'Local Boy Does Good – and Celtic!' may be an apt headline for Ferguson.

AT THAT TIME

In England, there was carnage on the road after a 90-vehicle pile up on the M42.

Kavanagh QC and Film 97 with Barry Noman were among the choices on the television.

The new Escort Azura car was on sale for a price of £10,495.

In the cinema, The English Patient was the pick of the current films.

Meanwhile, it was claimed that Scots had the lowest average hourly rates, with female bar-staff typically getting £3.50 per hour, considerably less than their counterparts elsewhere.

Ian Ferguson in action during an Old Firm clash in his final season at Ibrox.

DEREK McINNES

When Dick Advocaat arrived at Rangers, it appeared that the club would increasingly turn to foreign talent as an apparent dearth of good Scottish players limited signing options. The Dutchman embarked on a spending spree, bringing in players from all over Europe, but he retained within his squad the remnants of the Walter Smith era.

Derek McInnes had been signed in 1995 by the former Rangers boss for the paltry sum of £350,000, at a time when clubs could expect to shell out several millions for good quality midfielders. For many, it seemed that McInnes' signing would simply boost the Ibrox squad, but the young Scot proved more than capable of doing a job for Rangers. He helped the side to complete the historic 'Nine-in-a-Row' sequence and when others departed with Smith, McInnes remained, his fate uncertain.

Advocaat surveyed his resources and realised that McInnes could do a job for him. So, amidst a flurry of new signings, Derek McInnes remained as part of a small band of Scots players at Rangers. His appearances under Advocaat were limited, but he did show that whenever called upon, he could fit into the system with ease. In one Champions League match in particular, he filled an important role in nullifying the strike threat from the highly rated PSV Eindhoven front man Ruud van Nistelrooy.

When he finally left Rangers in 1999, he had over 60 appearances to his credit and celebrated that one decisive Championship success that completed the 'Nine'. He now plies his trade in England with West Bromwich Albion.

SCOTTISH PREMIER LEAGUE CHAMPIONSHIP
DUNDEE UNITED 0 RANGERS 1 (Laudrup)
Attendance: 12,000
Tannadice Park, Dundee — 7 May 1997

DUNDEE UNITED: Dykstra; McInally, McKimmie, Pressley, Perry;
Pedersen, Olofsson, Zetterlund (Dolan), McSwegan, McKinnon and McLaren (Winters).
RANGERS: Dibble; Cleland, Robertson; Petric, McLaren, Bjorklund, Moore,
Gascoigne (McInnes), Durie, Miller and Laudrup (McCoist).

L ike thousands of young Rangers fans through the years, Derek McInnes rejoiced as the team, bedecked in scarves and hats, celebrated Cup and Championship successes with the traditional lap of honour. To the strains of 'The Best', he watched and wished that some day he too could share in the joy of the players.

Despite making the professional grade at Morton and being acknowledged as one of the brightest young talents in the Scottish game, he never dared believe that his dreams of playing for Rangers could ever come true. For all his doubts, he had support from Morton boss, Alan McGraw, who considered that McInnes had a real chance of joining the 'Gers. McGraw believed that the youngster had the quality to do a turn for the Ibrox side, and told Rangers boss Walter Smith so on a number of occasions. As Smith looked to bolster his squad, he had McInnes watched and then made a move to secure the transfer. In 1995 Rangers paid Morton £350,000 for the services of the talented midfielder. It was a dream come true for Derek McInnes, but this was just the start.

That first season proved successful for 'Del', and he celebrated the club's eighth successive Championship in front of the joyous Ibrox crowd, but in this moment of victory there was a tinge of disappointment. He didn't play in the clincher and, although he took the plaudits of the fans, walking around the pitch with a club blazer instead of the blue jersey took the edge off things.

Next season, as Rangers edged towards the historic 'Nine-in-a-Row', Derek looked set to miss out again as he tried to fight back from injury. With a home match against Motherwell looking likely to be the title-clinching game, Derek was disappointed to find his name off the teamsheet. 'I had just trained after injury and the Gaffer probably thought that the 'Well game had come too quickly for me, but I was sad to miss that match,' recalled Derek.

'As you remember, however, things didn't go to plan that day [Rangers drew], and after the game we knew we had a tricky visit to Tannadice to contend with. The Gaffer turned and told me to bring my gear. We were heading up to St Andrews the following morning to prepare for the game. It seemed that I was in the frame.

'We were really focused for the game and Walter emphasised the importance of it all. As he said, the eight previous Championships would mean nothing if we couldn't win the coveted ninth. On the day of the game we waited anxiously for the team selection and around lunchtime the Gaffer read out the names. I was delighted to find that I had got a place on the bench.

'In a real gutsy performance we took control from the start and Laudrup got the vital opening goal that gave us the confidence that this would be our night. As the minutes ticked away through the first half and then late into the second, the Gaffer decided to pitch Ally McCoist and I into the fray for a taste of the occasion. I was hardly on the field one minute when the whistle went for full-time but, even with that limited contribution, I really felt part of it all. We were in ecstasy and, after we were presented with the Cup, we went across to the fans. I recalled those feelings when I was up in the stands as a young fan, but now my dream had come true. I was down there with a blue jersey on!

'After the game we headed to Glasgow, but stopped off at the Swallow Hotel in the outskirts of Dundee where the champagne was uncorked and the Gaffer proposed a toast. We had a few drinks and had a real party on the way back before reaching the city around midnight. We took the bus to George Square where around 2,000 fans had assembled. We gathered that there had been about 7,000 in the Square an hour earlier. After showing the trophy to the crowd we headed to Ibrox where another large group had gathered at the front doors.

'Inside the Stadium the party continued – probably for about three days actually!' laughed Derek. 'It was a great time and a real match to remember. For me it was more than that,' said Derek. 'It was a dream come true!'

AT THAT TIME

The headlines were dominated by talk of Labour's victory in the General Election, with the prospect of a Scottish Parliament at the forefront of debate.

In music, Michael Jackson was top of the charts with *Blood on the Dancefloor*.

In the cinema, *The Fifth Element* starring Bruce Willis was due for release, with *Space Jam* and *Liar, Liar* already topping screen lists.

In boxing, Prince Naseem Hamed made his first defence of his WBO and IBF featherweight titles against Billy Hardy, stopping his opponent in just 35 seconds.

Meanwhile, a beleaguered Celtic faced problems with Paulo Di Canio, with Fergus McCann insisting that his wayward star was going nowhere.

(Left to right) Paul Gascoigne, Derek McInnes,
Ally McCoist and Gordon Durie celebrate 'Nine-in-a-Row'.

DAVIE WHITE

Davie White was almost thrown into the manager's position at Ibrox amidst the turmoil that followed the sudden departure of Scot Symon in November 1967. White had arrived at Rangers with a great deal of credibility as a promising young coach, having served a very useful apprenticeship at Clyde. He introduced new training ideas to Rangers and was well respected among the players when Symon's dismissal catapulted him into a position that offered great opportunity, but an unenviable challenge. With Celtic revelling in the glory of their 1967 European Cup win, White faced an uphill task in overturning their Scottish dominance.

With a superb undefeated run until the last game of the Championship, he almost wrestled the title from Celtic, losing out on the final day. After just two years in the position, the Rangers board terminated his contract following a defeat in the European Cup Winners' Cup from up-and-coming Polish side Gornik Zabre. With more time at his disposal, he may have been able to turn the tide, but his appointment to the most difficult job in football was untimely. Not only did he have to contest with Stein's great Celtic side, Rangers themselves were in something of a transition with the glory days in the distant past.

Now, Davie White can only think of what might have been, but he is still proud to have held office at Ibrox. A regular visitor to the ground, his interest in the club is undiminished, as is his enthusiasm for the game. Who knows what he may have achieved had he been appointed some time later?

SCOTTISH FIRST DIVISION CHAMPIONSHIP
CELTIC 2 (Wallace 2) RANGERS 4 (Johnston 2, Penman, Persson)
Attendance: 75,000
Celtic Park, Glasgow — 14 September 1968

CELTIC: Simpson; Gemmell, O'Neil; Brogan, McNeill, Clark;
Johnstone, Lennox, Wallace, Connelly and Chalmers.
RANGERS: Martin; Jackson, Mathieson; Greig, McKinnon, Hynd;
Henderson, Penman, Jardine, Johnston and Persson.

The making of every Rangers manager has been their performance against old rivals Celtic, and Davie White perhaps more than most, as the youngest boss in the club's history, realised the importance of success against the other half of the Old Firm. After just ten months in the Ibrox hot-seat, following the dismissal of Scot Symon, White had survived his first encounter with Jock Stein's Celtic, emerging from Parkhead in the Ne'erday fixture with a creditable 2–2 draw. Although he failed to wrest the Championship from Celtic Park, he took Rangers into season 1968–69, brimming with confidence.

He had not added any major signings to his pool and was short of quality up front. Alex Ferguson was out of favour, Jim Forrest and George McLean had departed after the Berwick debacle that saw Rangers exit the Scottish Cup at the first hurdle 20 months earlier. However, Sandy Jardine had shown his versatility and gave White an option at centre-forward. In the opening game of the Championship, the midfielder-come-striker scored the Ibrox side's two goals in a win over Partick Thistle. With a visit to Celtic Park scheduled for the following week, White decided to persist with Jardine up front alongside the lightning-fast Willie Johnston.

The tactics worked a treat. Rangers got off to the perfect start with the opening goal coming just 15 minutes into the game. It was a goal made on the training field. White explained, 'We worked on getting players on the blind side of the defence with crosses swerved in low from the likes of Andy Penman. While the markers were picking up our taller players, Henderson, Johnston, and Persson would sweep in to latch onto these low crosses from the flanks. It worked well for the first goal with Persson getting on the end of a cross from Andy Penman.'

His tactical abilities never in question, White took great satisfaction from

Rangers' second goal, which came just two minutes later. 'We knew that if we could get Johnston on to the ball behind Celtic's Billy McNeill, dragging him forward out of the defence, John Clark could not live with his pace.' Again, the tactics succeeded when McNeill was drawn out of position and Willie Johnston was released with a superb pass from Andy Penman. John Clark had no answer to Johnston's pace and the Rangers player raced through before sliding the ball past Ronnie Simpson in the Celtic goal.

Rangers were 2–0 up and cruising, although Willie Wallace pulled a goal back for the Celts after 28 minutes. With the score at half-time 2–1, Rangers restored their two-goal advantage in 65 minutes through Penman. Wallace scored again for Celtic, but a last-minute goal from Willie Johnston sealed a 4–2 victory for Rangers. It was the Ibrox side's first win at Parkhead in almost five years.

For White, it was a memorable win, and one of a few highlights in a role that became increasingly difficult as Celtic continued their relentless domination of Scottish football. Although they went on to beat Celtic again in the Championship that season, points were frittered away against lesser sides, and two defeats and two draws in April put paid to Rangers' title hopes.

The next season was even more disappointing for White and Rangers as they failed to make any real impact on Celtic and then crashed out of the European Cup Winners' Cup. Davie White's reign was over after two years in the hottest seat in the game. However, there was no disgrace in failing to usurp a team that had won the European Cup and reached the final again two years later – the best side in Celtic's history. Indeed, for Rangers to defeat them twice in a season was no mean achievement.

White has every right to savour those victories, especially that cold September day in 1968 when the hard work in the training ground was rewarded. Nowadays, it is a time of reflection for the former Rangers boss, whose principal failing lay in being unable to match certainly the best side in Celtic's history. In many ways a man ahead of his time, he presided over a period of transition, when the days of the old-time manager were firmly discarded. In his short period at the helm he did, however, show glimpses of what might have been, had he been given the time that was ultimately denied him. None more so than in that fine victory at Celtic Park.

AT THAT TIME

The news was dominated by the plight of Biafra refugees and the hunger of children caught up in the war with Nigeria.

On television, *The Forsyte Saga* continued its great run on the BBC, while on ITV, John Cleese appeared in *The Auction Game*. On BBC 2, the popular American variety show *Rowan and Martin's Laugh-in* included John Wayne amongst the guests. In football, Scot Symon put aside his disappointment at leaving Rangers to take over as manager of Partick Thistle.

Motorists were attracted to the new Singer Gazelle, which cost £875.

In the cinema, movie-goers prepared for the premiere of *Chitty Chitty Bang Bang!*

Davie White watches his team in training.

GORDON SMITH

When Gordon Smith joined Rangers from Kilmarnock in 1977, there were some who turned up their eyebrows. He was a useful and exciting winger, but it appeared that Rangers were well covered in that department with Tommy McLean on the right and Davie Cooper on the left. However, manager Jock Wallace had other plans for Smith. He saw the pacy Smith as the ideal foil for Derek Johnstone in breaking from the midfield to support the striker. Between them, the Johnstone–Smith partnership scored 65 goals in season 1977–78, taking Rangers to the Treble for the second time in three years.

Smith's acquisition proved inspirational, and he helped the club to two Scottish Cups and two League Cups to add to that Championship success in 1978. He left Rangers for Brighton in 1980 and returned for a brief spell in 1982. In almost 160 games he scored 51 goals.

An articulate football pundit on television and radio, Smith is still closely involved in the game as a successful players' agent.

SCOTTISH PREMIER LEAGUE CHAMPIONSHIP
RANGERS 3 (Johnstone, Smith 2) CELTIC 2 (Edvaldsson 2)
Attendance: 48,788
Ibrox Stadium, Glasgow – 10 September 1977

RANGERS: McCloy; Jardine, Miller; Forsyth, Johnstone, MacDonald (McLean);
McKean, Russell, Parlane (Greig), Smith and Cooper.
CELTIC: Latchford; McGrain, Lynch; Edvaldsson, MacDonald, Casey;
Doyle, Dowie (McAdam), Glavin, Burns (Lennox) and Wilson.

G ordon Smith made immediate friends with Davie Cooper when he joined Rangers from Kilmarnock in 1977. Always keen on a 'punt', Cooper took odds on new-start Smith beating goalkeeper

Peter McCloy over 220 yards after training one day. Smith recalled, 'Jock Wallace had told me when I signed that he would not introduce me to the side until I had reached the fitness of the rest of his players. So, I was on the bench for the first match, but "Coop" knew I was pretty fast and fit because we had a strict training regime at Kilmarnock. The players called McCloy "Juantorena", after the great Cuban athlete because he had this big ranging stride and could shift.

'After training I was in the shower and "Coop" had been taking odds on me beating Peter, the notes were flying in. When I came out of the shower, I was told to get my gear back on and get out to the track. So off Peter and I went. At the trackside, Peter asked if I wanted the outside or inside lane. I got a little psychological advantage when I told him that the outside was fine, and then I went on to win the race by about 20 yards. From then on I was Davie Cooper's pal as he took in about three or four hundred pounds,' laughed Smith.

'Jock Wallace pulled me in after the race and said that I was in the side for the next game. I asked him if that was a normal training session we had just been through at Ibrox. When "Big Jock" said that it was, I told him it was just like the warm-ups we had at Rugby Park! The big man was in stitches.

'I had known Rangers were tracking me for about four years because Derek Johnstone had kept me informed, but it was a great day when it happened. When I signed, Jock said that he was well covered with wingers – he had Cooper, McLean and McKean – but he thought I could score goals from a forward midfield role. It was amazing because it was entirely the way I saw the type of role I could play. I had told the coaches at Rugby Park so many times, but it seemed I was destined to remain a winger.'

In his first start for Rangers, Smith did indeed seem to confirm the thinking he shared with Wallace. He scored two goals against Partick Thistle at Firhill. The following week, Rangers were scheduled to play the first Old Firm match of the season.

'I can remember the build-up was so different from any other game I had been used to. The papers were full of it all week and many people fancied Celtic because they had romped the Championship in the last season. On the night before the game I was apprehensive and excited, but not nervous. I never really got nervous for matches. Next day I arrived for the game and we went through our usual routine. There were no nights away in a hotel or anything like that then. Just before kick-off, Tommy Craig, who was the Rangers physio at the time, said that I should go down the tunnel to experience the atmosphere. He told me that it would prepare me better so that it wouldn't hit when I eventually went on to the field. I took his advice and it helped. Some of the fans in the enclosure saw me and cheered which give me a bit of a lift.

'When I eventually went out for the match I was so excited. I just kept thinking that my moment in football had arrived. This was really it – I could never have imagined as a youngster that I would play in this game, but here it was. It was the game I always wanted to play in but didn't dare believe that it would happen.

'The first half turned out badly for us in the game and we went two down to goals from "Shuggie" Edvaldsson. We had been playing quite well up to that game, but things just didn't work out in that first half. When we came in at half-time, I expected that we would get slaughtered, but Jock Wallace said that we were the better team and didn't deserve to be behind. Crucially, he told Derek Johnstone, who was playing centre-half, that he was moving him forward into attack.'

The move worked a treat. When Johnstone moved forward, Edvaldsson, who had proved such a threat in the air to Rangers, moved into defence to cover him. Smith immediately started to see opportunities and Rangers got a breakthrough in 53 minutes.

'Derek had a great touch and when the ball came through he flicked it into my path about 12 yards out. I hit the ball well and it sailed past Peter Latchford into the net. It was an incredible feeling scoring in my Old Firm debut, but we hadn't finished. Derek got an equaliser about 20 minutes later and then with less than ten minutes left Latchford fumbled a ball from Bobby Russell. It landed at my feet and I prodded it into the net.'

Rangers had achieved one of the most remarkable Old Firm reverses and Gordon Smith had more to celebrate than most with two goals. 'You just can't get much better than that for a player, scoring twice against Celtic on my debut. Even talking about it now sends tingles down my spine. It was an incredible feeling.'

The match confirmed that Smith had great potential in the midfield, and the lethal combination with Johnstone was a sign of the times ahead. 'We played three up front from then, with Cooper and McLean on the wings, and Derek Johnstone in the middle. I played in the middle of midfield, with Bobby Russell and Alex MacDonald on each side. Bobby and I just played football, but Alex put in a tremendous work-rate for us. The system worked well and Derek and I scored 65 goals between us that season as we went on to win the Treble. I also scored in the League Cup final against Celtic, which was another memorable match.'

Smith scored 27 goals that 1977–78 season and followed up with 18 in the next season – not a bad strike rate for a midfielder! It was a great season for the popular Rangers player and one in which no one with any sense would have bet against Smith and Rangers succeeding. 'Coop' would have endorsed that!

AT THAT TIME

It was reported from Uganda that President Idi Amin was in a coma after an operation.

Wimpey Homes in Baberton, Edinburgh, were on sale from £14,000.

On television, Jimmy Tarbuck presented *Winner Takes All* on ITV with *I, Claudius* on BBC 2.

In sport, George Best flew back to America as a wrangle continued between Fulham and Los Angeles Aztecs over his contract.

In motor racing, only a year after a near-fatal crash, Niki Lauda looked set to take the Formula One World Championship.

Gordon Smith in action for Rangers.

JIMMY MILLAR

It is a testament to the impact that Jimmy Millar made to Rangers when Walter Smith, himself something of a Rangers legend, speaks quite openly about a player who was his boyhood hero. The former Edinburgh publican, who nowadays spends his time on the golf course or at Ibrox on match days, assisting with corporate hospitality, has every right to be considered one of the Rangers greats. Signed from Dunfermline Athletic in 1955 for the princely sum of £5,000, he was a half-back converted to a prolific striker by manager Scot Symon. A member of a succession of great sides that Symon produced, Millar formed an irrepressible strike partnership with Ralph Brand and together they were known as 'M&B'.

In 317 games for Rangers, he scored 162 goals, helping the side to three League Championships, five Scottish Cups and three League Cups; and he deserved more than the two caps he won with Scotland. A popular figure, he recalls those magical memories of happy days in the '50s and '60s before the Stein era at Celtic Park.

He left Rangers in 1967 to join Dundee United before hanging up his boots. After a short time in management at Raith Rovers he gave up the game to concentrate on his pub.

SCOTTISH CUP FINAL (REPLAY)
RANGERS 1 (Johansen) CELTIC 0
Attendance: 96,862
Hampden Park, Glasgow — 27 April 1966

RANGERS: Ritchie; Johansen, Provan; Greig, McKinnon, Millar;
Henderson, Watson, McLean, Johnston and Wilson.
CELTIC: Simpson; Craig, Gemmell; Murdoch, McNeill, Clark;
Johnstone, McBride, Chalmers, Auld and Hughes.

J immy Millar is one of the most unassuming characters you could ever
have the pleasure to meet. He has declined public interviews because
he feels he cannot speak in front of large audiences, but that is in fact
a fallacy. When he is encouraged to open up, there is hardly a funnier or
nicer man among the Ibrox old school. Indeed he has so many anecdotes
of a wonderful Ibrox career that he could more than fill the pages of this
book himself.

It all began at Ibrox for Millar back in 1955 when he signed for Rangers
from Dunfermline for a fee of £5,000. 'I was part-time at East End Park
and working as a plumber earning £7.50 a week when I joined Rangers.
My wages went up to £16 at Ibrox in that first year, but even when I left
in 1967 we were only getting £45 a week basic plus £5 bonus. It is a big
change nowadays with players getting £30,000 a week and more.'

Signed initially as a wing-half, Millar eventually moved into the centre-
forward role after a particularly successful tour of Denmark in 1959. He
went on to become part of one of the finest strike lines in the club's history.
First Alex Scott then Willie Henderson took the right-wing berth, but the
four others in the front five run off the tongue of every fervent Rangers fan
of the period – McMillan, Millar, Brand and Wilson.

Millar's partnership with Brand was legendary and the pair remain good
friends to this day. Millar had great admiration for his strike partner's
enthusiasm and desire to work at his game. 'Ralphie was ahead of his time
really. He would go in for extra training and would work away at things on
his own. Then I would join him and we worked at our partnership, playing
one-twos and making runs.'

The partnership broke up in 1965 when Brand moved to Manchester
City, and Millar also found his appearances becoming less frequent by then
as the young Jim Forrest and George McLean took the front-line roles. It
may have seemed to many that Millar's glory days were behind him, but
there was one Cup final left that would become particularly memorable in
the midst of many.

'I remember that great Scottish Cup final replay in 1966 particularly
fondly. The first game was drawn 0–0 and it wasn't much of a game. The
replay was played on the following Wednesday evening. We were
struggling for players and Celtic had a good side at that time.'

Indeed, Celtic showed just two changes from the team that would
eventually go on to win the European Cup a year later. Rangers had Millar
at left-half to accommodate McLean and Johnston up front. Millar faced
Jim McBride who was at inside-right for Celtic. 'As a half-back you were

in direct opposition to the inside-forward of the other side.' Typically, Millar would not be drawn on how he performed in that little personal contest because 'you must always respect the opposition', but you can take it that he fared better. It is one of the nice things about Millar. He won't criticise anyone.

'Match preparations were nearly always the same for these games. We didn't stay away overnight, but met up at the St Enoch Hotel before heading over to Hampden. We were pretty confident going into the match, but I remember that Celtic had most of the game. With 20 minutes to go, the ball broke out of the Celtic area to Kai Johansen and he hit it into the far side of the net. The game finished 1–0 for us. It was a great experience to win at that stage in my career, even though I had won a few Cup finals with Rangers before. I remember two years earlier the game against Dundee in the 1964 Cup final when I scored two goals, but the man of the match on that occasion was Dundee goalkeeper Bert Slater. He really kept them in it.

'But the 1966 final was special too. After the game we went back to the St Enoch hotel but there were no big celebrations for the players in these days. We were all good clean-living guys,' he laughed. 'It was a case of a post-match meal then heading off home to bed. Things certainly have changed nowadays, but, then, at Ibrox even the wives didn't get a cup of tea and a pie!'

Nevertheless, Millar has great memories of Ibrox and, although he feels the game is not as exciting nowadays as it was in his day, he still loves coming to Ibrox for corporate hosting. He is certainly a fans player and even his recollections of a late winner against Celtic in a Ne'erday derby reflect his awareness of the importance of a Rangers victory to the crowds who revered them. As he reflected on that game back in 1960 he recalled, 'When the ball went into the net, it was at the Rangers end. I remember all the bottles being tipped up and you could almost hear them say "Happy New Year, Jimmy".'

Millar gave them more than a few happy years – 13 years in all, in a great Rangers career.

AT THAT TIME

The news in Scotland was dominated with controversy over a BBC programme about Glasgow gang warfare.

In the charts, Dusty Springfield held the top slot with 'You Don't Have to Say You Love Me'.

On television, *This Man Craig* continued to run on the BBC.

In football, Dundee fans were furious that star Charlie Cooke was transferred to Chelsea.

Stanley Baxter was appearing at the Metropole Theatre.

Jimmy Millar in action for Rangers.

JOHN GREIG

How can a man who played 857 games for Rangers single out any match among the myriad in a glittering career? Here is a man who won five Championship medals, six Scottish Cup emblems, four League Cups, and a hat-trick of Trebles for the Light Blues. Add to that his 142 goals, of which 88 were scored in League matches, placing him high in our all-time scoring charts, and the two Player of the Year awards. Oh, and there is also the little matter of an MBE, and you get the picture.

Edinburgh-born John Greig joined Rangers in 1961 as an 18-year-old, making his début for the Light Blues later that year among some of the great legends from the Struth era. It was a fine education for the youngster who seized the opportunity of a regular place in the side after a sparkling tour of Russia in 1962. Playing alongside the likes of Caldow, Shearer, Millar, Brand and Baxter, John Greig became an integral part of the side that Scot Symon moulded and which dominated Scottish football in the early '60s.

He eventually graduated to captain the side and helped take it to the European Cup final in 1967. Faced with the growing dominance of Celtic, it appeared at times as if Greig almost single-handedly provided the resistance to the challenge from Stein's men. Through the troubled late-'60s, he was the rock upon which the team was built, demonstrating the character that is an integral part of a 'true Ranger'.

When Willie Waddell took over as manager in 1969, he saw Greig as the key to the rebirth of Rangers, and the rehabilitation was completed with the European Cup Winners' Cup win in 1972. It was an important success that helped to bring sunshine to Ibrox again after the disaster in 1971.

With Wallace, Greig won the Trebles in the '70s as Rangers dominated once again. However, his playing career was brought to a sudden end with the departure of Wallace and his own elevation to the manager's office. Although initially successful, it was not to be a happy period.

When he eventually returned as a PR executive in the '90s, it was almost as if the prodigal son had returned. For Greig, it was certainly a case of coming home.

SCOTTISH LEAGUE CUP
RANGERS 4 (Greig, Christie, Brand 2) AIRDRIE 1 (Storrie)
Attendance: 32,000
Ibrox Stadium, Glasgow — 2 September 1961

RANGERS: Ritchie, Shearer, Caldow, Stevenson, Paterson,
Baxter, Scott, Greig, Christie, Brand and Wilson.
AIRDRIE: Dempster, Shanks, Keenan, Rankin, Johnstone, McNeil,
Newlands, Storrie, Tees, Caven and Duncan.

They call him 'Ledge', short for 'Legend'. Officially known as 'The Greatest Ranger', following a fan poll a few years ago, it is hardly surprising that John Greig has risen to idol status in recent years. With a career stretching back to 1961, as player, manager and more recently as an assistant to manager Dick Advocaat, it must be difficult to highlight one single game as his most memorable match. Many would anticipate that the European Cup Winners' Cup win in Barcelona in 1972 would be his selected game, but, showing more than a hint of nostalgia, he highlighted one other game that 'sticks out in my mind above all others'.

'On 2 September 1961, I made my début for the Rangers first team in a League Cup sectional tie against Airdrie. We had already qualified for the latter stages from a section that also included Third Lanark and Dundee. I was drafted in at inside-right to replace Ian McMillan who was rested before our vital European Cup tie with AS Monaco a few days later.

'I should have made an appearance four months earlier against Third Lanark, but my hopes were dashed by injury, so I was excited when Scot Symon announced that I was in the side at last. As we waited in the dressing-room, Jimmy Baxter played head tennis with me to help me to relax. I was comfortable with the squad, however, because I travelled by train from Edinburgh each day with two of the regulars, Millar and Brand.

'These two were always ready to offer a word of advice during training and, when I eventually claimed my place in the team, they helped me a lot. They were a couple of father figures to me in these days but I also had great admiration for them as professionals. Both worked at their game and even as a pair they would often go out on the training ground to work on their strike partnership.'

It was indeed something of a tradition at Ibrox at the time that the older players would assist the youngsters in the nurturing process. The great standing that Greig has in the game, and his embodiment of the Ibrox traditions, is a testament to the help he had from his peers in these early days.

'Anyway, as we took to the field against Airdrie there was a healthy crowd of over 30,000 inside Ibrox. It is every young fan's dream to play professional football and to trot out there would have been enough, but the day held even more in store for me. With only ten minutes gone I opened the scoring. It was a dream début. We won the game 4–1, but even as I left the field, filled with pride, I scarcely realised that it was the start of a long and fruitful road with Rangers.

'Ian McMillan returned to the side after then, but I still managed to feature in 16 games and scored 8 goals. I was chuffed to deputise for a player of his calibre. He also helped me a lot in these early years because he was part-time and, as a youngster, I worked with him in training after the full-time players had gone.

'Next season I travelled to Russia with the squad and I made my breakthrough. I captured a regular place in the side and we went on to win the Championship and the Scottish Cup. I also managed to grab a few goals in these early days and, almost exactly a year after my début, I scored a hat-trick in a League Cup match against St Mirren at Love Street.

'As I look back, it doesn't seem like yesterday, but then again it hardly seems that four decades have passed. A lot has happened over that time and the club has changed in so many ways. I am proud to remain a part of it all.'

They call him the 'Legend'. Is there any wonder why?

AT THAT TIME

Scotland was left reeling from the worst thunder and lightning storm to hit in years as a complete power failure was experienced in Greenock, Port Glasgow and Gourock.

Rangers were gearing up for a stiff schedule with 9 games in 25 days planned.

On television, Alan Whicker talked of life in Australia in *Whicker Down Under* while *Bonanza* and *Flying Doctor* were the other top-rated shows.

In the cinema, *Guns of Navarone* was playing in the Gaumont to sell-out audiences, while well-known Rangers fan and comedian Lex McLean starred in his own show at the Pavilion Theatre.

In golf, America regained the Walker Cup with a young Jack Nicklaus in their side.

Other sports news included an announcement that Rangers would meet Eintracht in October, to open the new £50,000 Hampden floodlights.

John Greig shoots against Celtic at Hampden.

MARK HATELEY

Rangers fans are not known for their respect of reputation, particularly when a player does not appear to fulfil expectations. When Mark Hateley arrived at Ibrox in 1990, he had a scrapbook that showed goals in the San Siro for AC Milan, a Championship success in Monaco, and a famous goal for England against Brazil in the Maracana Stadium. He arrived at Rangers after a long lay-off through injury and, despite some solid appearances, failed to impress many of the Light Blues' followers. It did not help that he seemed to be displacing the popular Ally McCoist, but Hateley buckled down and slowly won over the support. By the time Rangers shaped up for a Championship decider with Aberdeen, Hateley was well accepted. Two goals from the imposing striker sealed a historic victory for manager Walter Smith's side and secured Hateley's position in the hearts of the Rangers faithful.

Five years on and Hateley added to his collection of Championships with a winner's medal for each season as the club moved towards 'Nine-in-a-Row'. When he left to join Ray Wilkins at Queens Park Rangers, it seemed that the chapter had closed on his Ibrox career. However, as the club neared the Holy Grail that was the ninth Championship, Walter Smith swooped to bring Hateley back to boost a squad depleted through injury. It was an inspired move and the striker battled to help Rangers seal the vital title win, playing a significant part in the goal that finally sunk Celtic.

By the time Rangers had finally drawn a line under his Ibrox career, Hateley had played over 220 first-class matches and scored 115 goals. He added two Scottish Cups and three League Cups to his five Premier League Championship medals and received the ultimate of accolades from the press and his fellow pros when they each awarded him the Scottish Player of the Year Award in 1994.

Born in England, but with experience in France and Italy, he could be excused for having divided loyalties, but Mark Hateley has never failed to reveal the club that he holds most dear – Rangers Football Club.

SCOTTISH PREMIER LEAGUE CHAMPIONSHIP
RANGERS 2 (Hateley 2) ABERDEEN 0
Attendance: 37,652

Ibrox Stadium, Glasgow — 11 May 1991

RANGERS: Woods; Stevens, Nisbet, Brown (McCoist), Cowan (Durrant); Hurlock, Spackman, Ferguson, Walters; Hateley and Johnston.

ABERDEEN: Watt; Wright, McKimmie, McLeish, Robertson, Grant, Van de Ven, Bett, Simpson, Gillhaus and Jess.

Mark Hateley had a dream first season at Monaco when he signed for the club from the little principality on the Cote d'Azur. He helped them to the Championship and the French Cup final, scoring 20 goals on the way. However, in a European Cup match the following October he sustained an injury that was to keep him out of the game for 18 months. When he regained fitness and was still in the rehabilitation stages, Graeme Souness stepped in to take him to Ibrox for a transfer fee of around £1 million.

Hateley went straight into the Rangers side, but the progress he made in recovering his sharpness after the long lay-off was not acceptable to a minority of Light Blues fans. Believing that he had replaced favourite Ally McCoist, who was confined to the bench, the big English striker got a bit of a rough ride in the early stages from a section of the crowd. Hateley recalled, 'Many fans reckoned I had replaced Ally, but it was actually Mo Johnston that had taken his place. Gradually they warmed to me, but even in these early stages I just put it to one side. As a seasoned professional I could cope with that.'

As the season progressed, the goals began to come for Hateley and the fans began to realise that he could offer a contrast to the penalty box player that McCoist essentially was. He was strong in the air, physical and had good touch. To many he was the ideal striker and he had the benefit of considerable experience in some of the best leagues in football.

With Hateley in harness, Rangers made steady progress as the 1990–91 season neared a conclusion, until they were hit with the shock resignation of Graeme Souness with just four games remaining in the title race. Souness' assistant Walter Smith was appointed to fill the breach and carry Rangers through the remaining matches of the term. Rangers won the first game under Smith's guidance but, as the club struggled with debilitating injuries, they lost their penultimate game at Fir Park, Motherwell. Meanwhile, Aberdeen, who were chasing hard in second spot, took over at the top of the table as the results knocked Rangers back into second on goal difference. With only one game remaining, ironically against Aberdeen at Ibrox, Rangers knew that only a win would be enough to give them the title. The Dons were the form team, but Rangers were at home. The match was finely balanced.

Hateley recalled the build-up. 'We had a lot of players out through injury, but we had great spirit with a lot of tough heads in the dressing-room. Players like "Bomber" [John Brown] just didn't know the word defeat. So, although we were far from at full strength, we were confident.

'It was a game I was looking forward to. I was going to be up against Alex McLeish who was a great international central defender. However, apart from the contest with McLeish, I looked forward to the fray with the keeper. In every game I went into I tried to win a battle with the goalkeeper from the outset. The Aberdeen game was no different and, inside the dressing-room before the start, I told Gary Stevens to put the ball under the bar. It would give me a chance to challenge Dons' keeper Michael Watt for the cross and test him out. Sure enough, Gary put the ball in there and we went up for it. It ended up with bodies everywhere!'

It is commonly accepted that Hateley did intimidate Watt by his sheer physical presence. However, the first real chance of the game fell to Aberdeen when Van de Ven broke through to be one on one with Rangers keeper Chris Woods. The Dons midfielder lofted the ball straight into Woods' arms and the chance was lost.

Hateley recalled, 'I could see their heads go down after that. An experienced professional will look for these kind of signs and that gave me an extra lift. At that level you have to take your chances or you will be punished and Aberdeen's chance probably went then. I slowly moved forward down the left flank working the ball with first Gary Stevens then Mark Walters. Mark was very tight on the wing, close to the line, with players beside him and slightly off balance when he managed to get a long diagonal punt into the box. I rose between Alex McLeish and David Robertson to get to the ball and head it into the net.

'It was such an important goal for me and for the team. For me, it was great to score what I'd call a classic type of goal for me. One of my strengths had been in the air and I had scored lots of goals like that. It was the kind of goal that symbolised my type of play and I took great satisfaction from it. It was confirmation to me that I had got back to where I was before injury.

I also felt I had really arrived with the fans too, although they had universally accepted me by then in any case. But the goal was so important to us. The first goal always is, but on that occasion it was vital for Rangers.'

Already severely depleted with injuries, Rangers suffered further with the loss of leg-break victim Tom Cowan. Hateley recalled, 'It really did highlight the spirit of that team, when so many players played with injuries and with some, like John Brown, taking injections to get him through the match. Early in the second half I got a second goal and we knew we were home and dry, but we still had a bit of the match to play out. I ended up at left-back, behind Terry Hurlock, and Coisty came on as sub, four stone overweight, with about 15 minutes to go,' he laughed.

'I would say that it was one of the greatest moments in my career without a doubt. Although I had scored about 15 goals up to that game, the match was a bit of a turning point for me. It also showed that we had great character in that side, which was the basis upon which the success of the team was to be built in the future.'

At the time, Mark Hateley could not have envisaged that he would win several more titles before leaving and then returning to Rangers six years later. His return marked a significant milestone in the history of Rangers as the club sealed its ninth successive championship.

Recently nominated as one of the stars of Rangers 'Greatest Ever Team', it is little wonder that Ibrox is his spiritual home.

AT THAT TIME

Winnie Mandela was sentenced to six years in prison by a South African court.

Les Dawson introduced his new BBC game show *Fast Friends*, while Bob Monkhouse offered *Bob's Your Uncle* on ITV.

A pack of 20 Superkings cigarettes cost £1.83.

In Scotland, Falkirk won the First Division Championship under manager Jim Jefferies.

No sooner had the dust settled on Rangers' victory, but there was speculation linking the club with Andy Goram.

Mark Hateley turns away in celebration after opening the
scoring against Aberdeen.

ALEX MacDONALD

There has scarcely been a more inspirational figure in a blue jersey than Alex MacDonald. Wearing his heart firmly on his sleeve, the little midfield dynamo was perhaps the best piece of business the club made when he signed from St Johnstone in 1968 for a fee of £50,000. After a slow start to his career, when he struggled to shine, he eventually became the playmaker in the midfield and a vital member of Willie Waddell's then Jock Wallace's sides through the '70s.

The pinnacle of his career was undoubtedly the 1972 European Cup Winners' Cup win over Moscow Dynamo in Barcelona. By the time he left the club in 1980 he had added three Championship medals, four Scottish Cups and four League Cups. One of the most underrated players in the game, he earned a solitary cap which failed to reflect his huge importance to Rangers. In over 500 first-class games he scored 94 goals, representing an excellent strike rate for a midfielder. Always a big-time player, many of his goals inevitably came in Old Firm matches, European ties, and vital cup games.

When he left Rangers to join Hearts as player-manager, the Tynecastle side were revitalised and, along with assistant Sandy Jardine, he came within a whisker of winning the Championship and Scottish Cup. He also took Airdrie to the Scottish Cup final, where he lost out to Rangers. However, he was always destined to return to the club of his affections in some capacity and now he assists in the corporate duties on match days.

EUROPEAN CUP WINNERS' CUP FINAL

RANGERS 3 (Stein, Johnston 2) MOSCOW DYNAMO 2 (Eschtrekov, Makovikov)

Attendance: 45,000

Nou Camp Stadium, Barcelona — 24 May 1972

RANGERS: McCloy, Jardine, Mathieson, Greig, D. Johnstone, Smith,
McLean, Conn, Stein, MacDonald and W. Johnston.

MOSCOW DYNAMO: Pilgui, Basalev, Dolmatov, Zykov, Dobbonosov (Gerschkovitch),
Zhukov, Baidatchini, Jakubik (Eschtrekov), Sabo, Makovikov and Evryuzhikbin.

Long before he wore the light blue jersey of Rangers, Alex MacDonald would duck into Ibrox as a youngster, to play on the field and score imaginary goals against Celtic, before running for the adulation of an imaginary crowd on the vast empty east terracing. He was often chased for his life by the caretaker, but for the young MacDonald, reared close to the Stadium, it was a dalliance with a dream to play for the club he loved.

Several years on the dream became a reality when Rangers boss Davie White pounced to acquire the young midfielder from St Johnstone. But it was no plain sailing for MacDonald in the early stages of his Ibrox career. He remembers, 'It took me two years to get to grips with the fact that I was playing for Rangers. I had to try to put it into the back of my head because I used up so much nervous energy that I was shattered before I even got on to the field. I just couldn't work it all out. I was playing out a dream, but couldn't get it into perspective.'

When he did eventually get it together under Willie Waddell and then Jock Wallace, Rangers began to see the real value in MacDonald. A superbly fit and tenacious midfielder, he was to become a vital part of the revived Rangers of the early '70s. He was the classic Rangers player, displaying all the character that Jock Wallace considered an essential part of the make-up. With the likes of MacDonald in harness, the future looked bright for Rangers. While Waddell worked on the team's consistency for the long-haul challenge of League football, he believed that Rangers were a match for any side in cup football.

They displayed their appetite for cup competition at the highest level in season 1971–72 when they fought through to the final of the European Cup Winners' Cup in Barcelona. Their opponents would be Moscow

Dynamo in what was Rangers third appearance in the final of the competition. Unlike earlier rounds, when they faced stern competition from France (Rennes), Italy (Torino), Portugal (Sporting Lisbon) and Germany (Bayern Munich), Rangers went into the game as favourites, although the Rangers management team took nothing for granted.

The preparation for the game was meticulous. MacDonald recalled, 'Willie Waddell and Big Jock [Wallace] knew how to take the pressure off players. They would tell you about the opposition in good time, but their man-management skills were excellent. Before we flew out to Spain we got part of the build-up, but we didn't really get into the detailed talk about tactics and the opposition until we were in Barcelona. The attention to detail was always excellent, with Jock giving up pictures of the guys we would face. We were well set for the game.

'After we left the hotel for the game by bus, we could see thousands of Rangers fans everywhere as we neared the Nou Camp Stadium. I had family and friends over and I was trying to fix them up with tickets, passing them out the windows when we arrived.

'When the game kicked off we were confident. I was not nervous because when you pull on that blue jersey you just feel wonderful. We were fit and ready and the crowd were unbelievable. They really helped us and we got a perfect start when Colin Stein opened the scoring early on. Rangers at that time just piled ahead when we got the first goal and our whole game was geared towards attack. When Bud [Johnston] added two more goals to take the score to 3–0, I felt that we were comfortable, but they pulled a couple of goals back, with their second one coming with five minutes left. It was the longest five minutes I remember as we played out time.

'It was hard for us because both John Greig and Alfie Conn were not 100 per cent fit and we were shattered in the Spanish heat: we were playing with heavy cotton jerseys. We had actually taken perforated jerseys with us, but Willie Waddell reckoned that they weren't the right colour of blue, so they were ditched.

'As the time moved on, we gave a free-kick away near the end and the crowd thought the referee's whistle signalled the end of the game. They poured on, but, of course, had to go off again. When the whistle did finally blow, the fans came on and it was a bit frightening for us, although it could not detract from our achievement. Leaving aside the trouble at the end when the police misjudged the situation, our fans were magnificent.

'The fact that we didn't get presented with the cup on the pitch didn't matter to me. What was more important was that we won it. When we got back to Glasgow we paraded it around Ibrox in the rain and I remember looking out and seeing the great former Rangers captain Bobby Shearer standing in among the crowd. That was very emotional and showed that once a Ranger, always a Ranger.'

If Rangers ever go on to emulate the feat of the boys of 1972 and the players parade the trophy around Ibrox Stadium, you can expect MacDonald to be there, just as Shearer was almost 30 years ago.

AT THAT TIME

In Alabama, Governor George Wallace sat up in bed as he recovered from the attempted assassination that left him paralysed from the waist down.

The Goodies was the top comedy show on BBC and Love Thy Neighbour was popular on ITV.

The future of a Clyde shipyard was secured when all parties reached agreement with Texan oil company Marathon for the fabrication of drilling and production platforms.

In the movies, the 24th Carry On film, Carry on Abroad, was released with Jimmy Logan in the cast alongside Barbara Windsor.

Elsewhere in sport, Northern Ireland shocked England at Wembley with a 1–0 win.

Alex MacDonald with former Rangers stars Willie Henderson (centre) and George Niven (right).

TREVOR STEVEN

There are not many players who can claim to have been Rangers' most expensive acquisition and their costliest export all within the space of 24 months, but Trevor Steven holds that almost unique honour. Signed from Everton in 1989 for a fee of around £1.7 million, the value decided by a tribunal, Steven made an immediate impact on Rangers, providing considerable skill and experience to the right midfield. He came to Ibrox with a solid career already behind him. At Goodison Park, he won the English First Division Championship and the FA Cup, and experienced European success with the European Cup Winners' Cup in 1985.

When he was at his peak during his spell at Ibrox, he was lured to Marseilles for a fee of around £5.6 million. When the French side, already discredited for malpractice, failed to fulfil payments on the transfer fee, Steven returned to Rangers. His return continued the love affair he had with the club, and he went on to help Walter Smith's men to the Championship in each of the following three seasons before recurring injury effectively ended his career in 1996.

A player of true class who went on to earn a total of 36 England caps, Steven added 4 Premier League Championships and 3 League Cups to his haul. Now he puts his experience in complex contract negotiations to good use as a registered players' agent. It maintains his close association with the game.

SCOTTISH PREMIER LEAGUE CHAMPIONSHIP
DUNDEE UNITED 0 RANGERS 1 (Steven)
Attendance: 15,995
At Tannadice Park, Dundee — 21 April 1990

DUNDEE UNITED: Main; Cleland, Krivokapic, Narey, Welsh, Jackson, McKinley, McInally, Paatelainen, French and Preston.
RANGERS: Woods; Steven, Gough, Butcher, Munro; Steven, D. Ferguson, Spackman, McCoist, Johnston and Walters.

W hen Trevor Steven joined Rangers in 1989, the conveyor belt of talent, which had traditionally carried players south of the border, had already been put firmly in reverse in the 'Souness Revolution'. The Rangers boss had swooped three years earlier for England internationals Terry Butcher and Chris Woods, and they were subsequently joined by Graham Roberts, Ray Wilkins, Mark Walters and others.

Steven recalls the period when the opportunity to join Rangers arose, but the Ibrox side had competition for his signature. 'I had the chance to join Manchester United and met Alex Ferguson on the Monday and Graeme Souness on the Tuesday. But I chose Ibrox because I was particularly impressed with the manager and I believed that it was the place to be at that time. There was great excitement surrounding Rangers Football Club generally and I would have the opportunity of playing in front of 45,000 every other week. Another factor was that there was no European football in England at that time following the Heysel Stadium disaster. Playing in Scotland gave me the opportunity to get back on that stage again. There was so much interest in the south in what was happening at Rangers. They had England captain Terry Butcher and a former England captain Ray Wilkins. The whole prospect of joining Rangers was exciting. I considered them to be the best team in the United Kingdom at that time.

'When I came up to complete the signing it was only the second time I had been in Glasgow. I had played there earlier for England in a 2–0 win at Hampden, but when I saw Ibrox for the first time I was very impressed. It was an excellent stadium.'

Steven settled in immediately at Ibrox, scoring on his début in a friendly against Tottenham Hotspur. With Ray Wilkins playing in the central midfield, Steven operated on the right flank, a position he was well familiar with. Although Rangers had a disappointing start to the League campaign with two defeats and a draw in the first three games, they quickly recovered and, with three games to play, had a chance to take the Championship at Dundee United's Tannadice Park. It was to be the setting for a game that Trevor Steven was to have fond memories of.

Steven recalled, 'We were virtually at full strength for the game, although Ray Wilkins had left to return to London four months earlier. I remember we settled into the game well and Mo Johnston and Ally McCoist were causing United a few problems. Then, with about 57 minutes gone, Stuart Munro carried the ball down the left wing and then crossed it into the box. I got in a run and then rose to connect really well with the ball and send it into the net for the only goal.'

It was a textbook finish from the English midfield player who timed his run and jump perfectly. 'Strangely, although I didn't score a lot of goals with my head, the ones that I did were generally pretty crucial ones.

'That goal was enough to give us the Championship and there was a great deal of satisfaction in it for me. I felt it was something of a payback time for Graeme Souness, who had brought me to Ibrox. I felt that I had been a real part of it all and had contributed to the success in my first season. The whole experience was a complete change for me, playing a different type of football, and the Championship win was really important.

'By the second year the team got even stronger and we were playing a typical British type of game. Indeed, we had no foreigners in the team as far as I can remember. It really was a team effort with no single player exerting influence over the side.

'Although I have selected this as my match to remember, there were other games I recall with relish, like the New Year victory over Celtic in 1993 at Ibrox when I scored the only goal, again with a header. But that Championship clincher against Dundee United was special and, although we didn't realise at the time, it was part of the march towards the "Nine-in-a-Row". The win at Tannadice gave us the second title in the run.'

The arrival of Trevor Steven at Ibrox was important for both the player and Rangers. A seasoned internationalist, his arrival consolidated the club's image as a progressive side capable of attracting the best. For Steven, it was a great opportunity to enjoy life at Ibrox during one of the most exciting periods in the club's history.

AT THAT TIME

In politics, Margaret Thatcher was under fire from the opposition over the Iraqi Supergun fiasco, after it was revealed that a British firm had exported vital components.

In Hollywood, it was reported that 58-year-old Elizabeth Taylor was fighting for her life following a bout of pneumonia.

While Rangers celebrated their victory in the Championship, Gary Stevens prepared to get married.

On television, a different perspective on life at a football club was offered in the drama serial, *The Manageress*.

In football, Liverpool topped the English First Division with Manchester United languishing in 14th place.

Trevor Steven in action against Marseilles, the team
he was later to join.

WILLIE JOHNSTON

There has rarely been a more colourful figure at Ibrox than Willie Johnston. Signed in 1964 from Fife junior football, the precocious winger quickly graduated to the first team and played alongside some of the great Ibrox heroes of the Symon era, including Baxter, Greig, Henderson, Caldow, Shearer and Millar, before carving out his own niche in Rangers' history. The pinnacle of his career, during which he put together almost 400 first-class appearances and scored 125 goals, came in the European Cup Winners' Cup final in 1972. Johnston scored two of Rangers' three goals to give the Light Blues the trophy – at the third time of asking. Having played in a losing final against Bayern Munich five years earlier, the victory was particularly sweet.

A firebrand character, his career was frequently interrupted by suspension and his international career was tainted in Argentina in 1978 when he was sent home after having failed a drug test which detected illegal, but not potent substances. Irrepressible as ever, however, Johnston put the disappointments behind him to continue an excellent career which also took him to England and Canada. He ended his career at Heart of Midlothian, with an enviable collection of medals. During a two-spell Rangers career, punctuated by eight years away from the club through much of the '70s, he won one Scottish Cup medal and two League Cups apart from that famous Barcelona win.

He is now a publican in Kirkcaldy, Fife, but still makes frequent visits to Ibrox where he is well received by the club and fans alike.

EUROPEAN CUP — SECOND ROUND, SECOND LEG
RAPID VIENNA 0 RANGERS 2 (Forrest, Wilson)
Attendance: 70,000
Prater Stadium, Vienna — 8 December 1964

RAPID VIENNA: Veres; Zaglitsch, Hoeltt; Skocik, Glencher, Hasil; Schmid, Wolny, Grausam, Floegl and Seitl.

RANGERS: Ritchie; Provan, Caldow; Greig, McKinnon, Wood; Johnston, Millar, Forrest, Baxter and Wilson.

W illie, or 'Billy' Johnston, as he prefers to be known, was one of the great characters of football. No other player has gone to the touchline to take a corner and engaged in negotiations with a fan over the sale of a garden shed, as he once did while at West Bromwich Albion! Fans on the trackside at Ibrox would regularly tell of the off-the-cuff quips from the Rangers winger as he went out to the touchline to take throw-ins. In a sense, the interaction helped consolidate a bond that developed between Johnston and the supporters wherever he played. However, there was much more to the player than his sense of humour and quick turn of phrase. He was one of the most exciting forwards to wear the light blue of Rangers in the post-war era.

Nicknamed 'Bud' after he turned up for training wearing a long fur coat like one worn by the English music hall artist Bud Flanagan, Johnston graduated to the first team in 1964. Although Scot Symon's great team of the early '60s was already on the wane, he benefited from the experience of playing alongside the likes of Jimmy Millar, Bobby Shearer and Jim Baxter, all established Rangers legends in their own right.

Though the later part of the decade was troubled for Rangers, he remained one of the shining lights in a team desperate to restore the club to dominance in Scotland. When Willie Waddell took over as Ibrox boss in 1969, he saw Johnston as a key player who had the versatility to play either on the flanks or through the middle. Waddell had immense faith in Johnston who played a vital role in the rehabilitation of Rangers, culminating in the famous 1972 European Cup Winners' Cup win in Barcelona. It was a personal triumph for the player who scored two of Rangers' three goals, and it could be assumed that this would be his most memorable match. However, in typical unselfish manner, he was more keen to recall a game in which a teammate pulled out a sparkling show.

He recalled, 'I will always remember the away tie against Rapid Vienna in 1964. It was the best I have ever seen Jim Baxter playing. He was immense and strolled through the match, but with about five minutes to go he nutmegged one of the Austrians, then did it again and the guy lunged at him. It was a terrible tackle and we knew that it was a bad injury. Jim himself said that as soon as it happened he knew that his leg was broken. He wouldn't let the physio touch it.

'It was a tragic end to my first-ever European tie. I had played in the first leg at Ibrox three weeks earlier when we got a 1–0 win. I had only made my début about a month before. With the second leg only a couple of days away, Scot Symon called me and said, "Billy, you're playing outside-right." I told him I had never played outside-right, but he had made up his mind what he wanted me to do. At that time we weren't really given any tactic talks. We were just expected to get on with it.

'We assembled at Ibrox then travelled to the airport for the flight to Vienna, but for a time it looked touch and go for the match with the city covered in snow. The game went ahead, though, and I played well. Because I wasn't entirely comfortable on the right, Davie Wilson switched wings with me. We got a good start when Jim Forrest scored after about 20 minutes and as Jim [Baxter] ran the game from there we got more and more chances. Early in the second half I broke clear and then cut the ball back for Wilson, who scored the second.

'It was 3–0 in aggregate and we were just cruising after that with Jim at the centre of everything. Then in the final minutes he took that tackle. The Austrian wasn't even sent off!

'Baxter's injury took the shine off the result for everyone, but when we got back to the hotel it was quite different. There was a party around Jim's bed! I remember there was a bottle of Dimple whisky getting passed around as we all gathered around Jim, while his plaster was still wet! It was an experience for a youngster, but these guys were all good professionals and Jimmy Millar looked after me.

'Next day, because of the snow, we couldn't fly out of Vienna so we had a six-hour bus journey to Strasbourg. There was no shortage of entertainment on the way. Andy Stewart and the Alexander Brothers were on our bus and they kept the singing going all the way!

'After that game I really felt part of it all. As I said, I had already played a few games, but to play in an away European tie was special. Strangely, I wasn't a Rangers fan as a youngster. I was brought up in Ruchill and I was a keen Partick Thistle fan. I used to go to a lot of the games through the '50s, when they had a good side. But when I joined Rangers and got more involved in the team my devotion went to them.'

It was ironic that Davie Wilson should switch wings with Johnston during the match in Vienna because the youngster was to claim the position on a more permanent basis shortly after the game. Wilson's days had almost come and gone, but Billy Johnston was a more than capable replacement. Vienna was just a taste of things to come for Rangers – a European experience that was to blossom in Barcelona almost eight years later.

AT THAT TIME

On television, *Coronation Street* topped the viewing charts, with *Steptoe and Son* a short distance behind.

In football, Hearts were the leaders of the Scottish First Divison with Chelsea holding the top spot in England.

In the cinema, audiences were eagerly awaiting the premiere of *Mary Poppins*, starring Julie Andrews and Dick van Dyke, while in the Regent Cinema, *Zulu* was playing to a full house each evening.

Politicians were calling for an inquiry into a typhoid outbreak that hit Aberdeen.

For those who like a tipple, a 40 oz bottle of fine Spey Royal whisky was on sale in off-licences for 65 shillings.

Jim Baxter, who tragically suffered a broken leg during
the match against the Austrians.

TOMMY McLEAN

When Willie Waddell returned to revitalise Rangers after the departure of Davie White in 1969, he had little hesitation in moving to acquire Tommy McLean from Kilmarnock. He had nurtured the youngster's career at Rugby Park a few years earlier and always admired his tenacity and passing. A modern-style winger, McLean's game was more about pinpoint passes and crosses, especially from dead-ball positions, than surging runs and jinking moves along the touchline. He was to prove a vital part of Waddell's resurgent side and Jock Wallace's Treble teams of the '70s, providing a steady supply of dangerous crosses to the aerial strengths of the likes of Derek Johnstone, Derek Parlane, and Colin Jackson.

Signed for just £65,000, McLean went on to have 12 successful seasons at Ibrox during which he played over 450 games and scored almost 60 goals. He won three Championships, four Scottish Cups and three League Cups with Rangers to add to his Championship win with Kilmarnock in 1965. However, the pinnacle of his success at Rangers was the European Cup Winners' Cup win in 1972 against Moscow Dynamo.

When he left Ibrox in 1983 he showed real managerial talents, leading Motherwell to the Scottish Cup in 1991. After a period out of the game, he recently returned to Rangers to head up Rangers' youth coaching at the new training ground, Murray Park.

SCOTTISH FIRST DIVISION CHAMPIONSHIP
RANGERS 3 (Johnstone, McLean, Parlane) CELTIC 0
Attendance: 70,000
Ibrox Stadium, Glasgow – 4 January 1975

RANGERS: Kennedy; Jardine, Forsyth, Jackson (Miller), Greig; McDougall, Johnstone, MacDonald; McLean, Parlane and Scott (Young).
CELTIC: Hunter; McGrain, McNeill, McCluskey, Brogan; Glavin, Hood (Johnstone), Murray; Callaghan, Dalglish and Wilson.

Tommy McLean may not have scored many goals in his 11-year Ibrox career, but his contribution to the impressive tallies accumulated by the likes of Derek Johnstone and Derek Parlane is immeasurable. Unlike Willie Henderson, who he followed into the Rangers number 7 jersey, McLean was not typical of the wingers of the '60s. Like the others, he patrolled the right flank, but his game was more about accuracy of delivery in his crosses than a sprint to the touchline. Willie Waddell was well aware of McLean's creativity when he signed him for Rangers. As boss of Kilmarnock he had nurtured the youngster in a solid Championship-winning side in 1965.

McLean rewarded Waddell for his faith in him by helping Rangers to the European Cup Winners' Cup in Barcelona in 1972. The winger provided the cross that gave Willie Johnston the vital second goal. It helped consolidate McLean's position with the Rangers fans as Henderson was confined to the history books, and there was greater appreciation of what the little winger could offer.

The victory in Barcelona was momentous, but the fans were desperate to see the Championship flag fly once again over Ibrox. It had been 11 years since Rangers had won the title, but Waddell and then Jock Wallace had steadily rehabilitated the side. By season 1974–75 there was some optimism that the team could prove that they were more than just a cup team. It was Waddell himself who first suggested that the team had not reached the consistency required to take the Championship but, as January 1975 approached, Rangers were just two points behind Celtic with the annual New Year fixture coming up.

McLean recalled, 'I stayed in Larkhall, which you could say was a bit of a Rangers stronghold, so there was always immense interest in the Old Firm game from about the Monday before the match. When I was out and about people would keep urging, "Make sure you beat the Celtic on Sunday."

'It was always a fixture that I loved to be involved in and one that I really miss to this day. I was pretty fortunate too that I could prepare for the game early on, knowing that I would probably be in the team. I was regularly in the side, so there wasn't the same anxiety that some felt as to whether they were in or not.

'Going into the match I was quite nervous, as I always was, but that didn't really affect me. When you get on the pitch you know what you have to do. I knew that I would probably be up against Celtic's Jim Brogan. I had a deep-lying wing role that allowed me to pick up the ball deep and move more penetratively forward. Brogan would tend to follow me everywhere, picking me up deep and also matching my runs.

'In our team that day we had Colin Jackson, Derek Johnstone, Derek Parlane and Ally Scott who were all good in the air, so I would be looking to get crosses in for these guys. As usual, when the match kicked off the atmosphere was tremendous. Early on I felt good and I sensed it could be our day. We got a great start when I curled over a cross for Johnstone to score past Ally Hunter in the Celtic goal. The first goal was always vital in an Old Firm game and we were obviously delighted to make the breakthrough. These games are always finely balanced and although the first goal is often enough for victory, you can never really be comfortable until you get a second.

'It was 1–0 at half-time, but just after the break I scored the second. I took a pass from Alex MacDonald and ran down the right then unleashed a shot with my left foot. It was my first goal against Celtic and a great feeling. I was on top of my game and we were well in control. It is a great feeling being on top with a good lead in these matches, but we continued to push ahead. With less than 15 minutes to go we added a third and again I had a hand in it. I curled a cross over into the box and Parlane got on the end of it to make it 3–0. It completed a memorable match for me in many respects. Getting my first goal against Celtic and having a hand in the other two made it a bit special.'

It was Rangers' biggest win over Celtic in 12 years and it was to be vital as the victory drew them level with Celtic in the title race. By the end of February they had gone four points clear and were boosted by the return of Colin Stein who arrived on an £80,000 transfer from Coventry City. Celtic fell away after their Ne'erday defeat, leaving Hibernian as the only real challengers and the title was eventually decided at Easter Road. A goal from Stein was enough to give Rangers the point they needed for the Championship. It ended a long barren spell without the League Flag, but once again it would fly over Ibrox. For McLean there was the satisfaction that he had played a vital role, appearing in all but one of the League fixtures, and then there was that special Old Firm win. It was the beginning of a great period for Rangers, ending in two Trebles with McLean at the heart of it all.

Ironically, five of his six Scotland caps came when he was at Kilmarnock. Grossly underrated at international level, he was one of the finest wingers to play for Rangers.

AT THAT TIME

Britain was in the midst of massive industry strikes and the Prime Minister Harold Wilson warned workers they could lose their jobs.

On television, John Alderton was popular in *No, Honestly* while BBC showed war drama *Colditz*.

A housebuilder advertised new semi-detached villas in Bothwell for just under £9,000.

Drivers were shocked at the news that petrol could soar to £1 per gallon.
In the cinema *Airport 1973* was showing at most of the major venues.

Tommy McLean in a familiar joust with Celtic's Jim Brogan.

JOHN McGREGOR

John McGregor played with both Rangers and Liverpool, but there will always be a sense that his true potential was never fulfilled as a result of frequent and debilitating injuries. A tough central defender, he joined Liverpool straight from Queens Park at a time when both Celtic and Rangers were tracking his career. It was during his time at Anfield that he came to the attention of Graeme Souness, who snapped him up for Ibrox when he was freed by the English side.

McGregor added steel and versatility to Rangers and comfortably slotted in beside Graham Roberts and Terry Butcher, but his career was punctuated with knee injuries. Although he laboured on through later seasons, he never managed to attain the regular fitness necessary to maintain his place in the side and was eventually forced to retire while still in his twenties. However, he can look back on that first exciting season at Ibrox when he managed 32 appearances, playing an important role in some famous victories against the likes of Dynamo Kiev and Aberdeen in the League Cup final in 1987.

When his career ended, the statistics show that he played 34 games for Rangers and won that solitary League Cup medal. Who knows how his career may have developed but for injury, but he puts that aside nowadays as he helps the Rangers Under-21 side progress. Coaching can never replace playing, but for McGregor there is the satisfaction in seeing the new Rangers talent emerge under his guiding hand.

SCOTTISH LEAGUE CUP FINAL

RANGERS 3 (Cooper, Durrant, Fleck) ABERDEEN 3 (Bett, Falconer, Hewitt)

Attendance: 71,961

Hampden Park, Glasgow — 25 October 1987

RANGERS: Walker; Nicholl, Munro, Roberts, Ferguson (Francis), Gough,
McGregor (Cohen), Fleck, McCoist, Durrant and Cooper.
ABERDEEN: Leighton; McKimmie, Connor, Simpson (Weir), McLeish,
W. Miller, Hewitt, Bett, J. Miller, Nicholas and Falconer.

With his career punctuated with injury, there is a tinge of regret as John McGregor savours the memories of some of the great games he played in. It is a matter of speculation as to how many medals he would have added to his career but, in being a part of the scene at Ibrox during the great Souness era, he would have expected to have shared in at least some of the glory that others enjoyed. However, his time at Ibrox was hardly fruitless. It provided him with an eventful and ultimately emotional moment at Hampden as Rangers took on Aberdeen in the 1987–88 League Cup final.

He recalled, 'I had been playing well in the run-up to the game, and the week before, we had salvaged a point against Celtic when Goughie scored in the last minute after we had been 2–0 down, with Graham Roberts having to take over in goal when Chris Woods went off. I had never played in a major Cup final before so I was hoping to be in, but I wasn't sure how Souness would play it. Terry Butcher was out so it strengthened my call but Gough and Roberts were also available.

'When we got to the ground the team was announced about an hour and a half before kick-off. I was delighted to find that I was in the team and Souness told me I would play in the inside-left position, just inside Davie Cooper. However, he wanted me to play in a marking role, picking up the Dons' Jim Bett.

'It was quite even early on and then Aberdeen scored through Bett with about eight minutes gone. For a moment I thought that the whole occasion might go pear-shaped for me. They had a good team at that time with the likes of McLeish, Miller and Bett, of course. But it didn't take us long to get level. We got a free-kick just outside the box and Davie Cooper took it. I think everyone knows the rest about that one. It was the hardest and

170

straightest free-kick I have ever seen. "Coop" saw the gap and hit it into the top corner of the net. Jim Leighton in the Aberdeen goal later said he nearly got to it, but "Coop" commented that he only nearly got to it when it was bouncing back out of the net!

'We made it 2–1 with a goal through Durrant who played a great one–two with McCoist. Then they equalised and went 3–2 up in the second half, before Robert Fleck got a late equaliser for us. At 3–3 and just before the end I had a great chance. The ball came out to me on the edge of the box and just as I was about to hit it, it bobbled and I put it over the bar. Even now I think about that moment, because nine times out of ten I would be confident of scoring. I could have won the cup with that goal.

'The match went into extra-time and was becoming stretched, with chances coming at both ends. Then Willie Miller put a heavy challenge in on me, which caught me on my bad leg. I thought at first it was broken and my knee also seemed to be away again. I was stretchered off and taken into the dressing-room but by the time I got in there I felt fine. The Doc looked at it and said it just needed about nine or ten stitches which he attended to, but when I told him I wanted to go out to watch the game from the dugout he told me to stay where I was. He didn't want me putting any pressure on the leg. David Holmes, who was chairman at that time, came down to see how I was.

'I listened to all the noises of the crowd and then the match went in to extra-time and penalties. One of our backroom boys kept me in touch with what was happening all the way through, running in and out of the dressing-room with the details. Then I heard a big cheer, which I knew meant that they had missed a penalty, before a huge roar when we won with the final kick. I told the Doc I was going out, but he still told me to stay there. I just looked at him and told him that I was going – he wasn't going to stop me. This was a big moment for me.

'I hobbled down the tunnel and out on to the pitch where everyone was celebrating. I went up for my medal and then went round the pitch with the Cup with my shirt on, not my football jersey. My mother still has the group photograph on the wall and I do regret that I didn't have my jersey on, but I had my medal and no one could take that away from me.

'It was a dream come true and, although I didn't finish the game, it was a magical experience.' It was a real match to remember.

AT THAT TIME

The headlines were made by five-month-old Kaylee Davidson who became Britain's youngest-ever heart transplant survivor.

In sport, Frank Bruno defeated Joe Bugner in the eighth round in a fight that failed to live up to expectation.

On television, *Bread* was popular on BBC with Rik Mayall providing the laughs on ITV's *The New Statesman*.

In the cinema, youngsters were attracted to Disney's latest offering *The Rescuers*, which was showing at most venues.

In England, Tottenham Hotspur boss David Pleat resigned after new allegations emerged about his private life.

An injured John McGregor, watched anxiously by Ally McCoist.

COLIN JACKSON

There are few players who have shown as much devotion and loyalty to Rangers as the imposing Colin Jackson. Signed in 1963 as a 17-year-old from Sunnybank Athletic in Aberdeen, the central defender served a long apprenticeship in the reserves before he finally got the chance to secure a regular place in the side in season 1970–71, when Ronnie McKinnon finally gave up the number 5 shirt. His patience was rewarded as he became an integral part of the resurgent team that Willie Waddell moulded, then he became the anchor of Jock Wallace's successful Treble teams in the '70s.

Despite his successes, which included three Championships, three Scottish Cups and five League Cups, one of the lowest points in his Rangers career came when a training ground injury deprived him of his place in the club's European Cup Winners' Cup win in Barcelona. Jackson put the disappointment aside to go on and add eight international appearances to his growing Ibrox career. By the time he finally left Rangers in 1982, he had played over 500 first-class games for the club and scored 40 goals.

Like many of his contemporaries, Jackson still turns up at Ibrox on match days to assist in hosting the corporate entertainment. Always a popular figure, he never wearies of chatting with the guests, many of whom well remember those heady days when Jock Wallace's side dominated Scotland.

SCOTTISH LEAGUE CUP FINAL
RANGERS 2 (MacDonald, Jackson) ABERDEEN 1 (Davidson)
Attendance: 60,000
Hampden Park, Glasgow — 31 March 1979

RANGERS: McCloy; Jardine, Dawson; Johnstone, Jackson, A. MacDonald; McLean, Russell, Urquhart, Miller, Smith and Cooper (Parlane).
ABERDEEN: Clark; Kennedy, McClelland; McMaster, Rougvie, Miller: Strachan, Archibald, Harper, Jarvie, Davidson (McLeish).

B y the time Colin Jackson took to the Hampden pitch in March 1979 against a good Aberdeen side, he had already played in seven major finals for Rangers and won five of them. However, the League Cup final in season 1978–79 was destined to be a little more personal and special for the tall central defender. It is every player's ambition to play in a Cup final, but to score the winning goal in the dying seconds is the stuff of dreams. But that is exactly how the game unfolded for Colin Jackson in a match that he recalls vividly to this day.

'Aberdeen were a good side at that time and were certainly on the up. They had a blend of youth and experience with some fine young players coming through. Up front they tended to play with two strikers, Steve Archibald and Joe Harper, who were a bit of a handful. I tended to pick up Harper in these games, and we always had a good barney. There was always a good bit of talking during the game but we got on pretty well off the field. In fact, occasionally I would go for a drink with wee Joe and some of the other Aberdeen players, including Derek MacKay, who scored against Celtic in a Scottish Cup final win for the Dons, and Jimmy Smith.

'In the middle of the field they had Gordon Strachan, who was a little dynamo, but we had a fair side too. In the previous year we had won the Treble, but Jock Wallace had resigned to be replaced by John Greig. We were ahead in the League and still in both cups, so we had a real chance of achieving back-to-back Trebles.

'We were just about at full strength, as were Aberdeen. They had a young Alex McLeish on the bench and Willie Miller in their defence.

'I can remember that the game was quite even and they maybe had the slightly better team. They took the lead about 15 minutes into the second half and for a spell it looked as if we might lose, but we started to get a grip on the game and exerted some pressure. By this time Alex McLeish had come on as substitute and started to pick me up at corners and free-kicks. Then, with about a quarter of an hour to go, Alex MacDonald got the equaliser. We kept pushing forward and I remember that in the dying minutes I got in a tangle with Steve Archibald. His finger gouged my eye as we tussled for the ball, but it was an accident. I couldn't really see out of it as we broke upfield and then got a free-kick out on the right.

'Because the game was near the end I started to head up into the box, but as I was running I still couldn't get good vision until I got to the halfway-line when it started to clear. I ran up to the back of the box and as Wee Tam [McLean] prepared to take it I made a run and got on the blind side of McLeish. I am sure that in later years, when he got more experienced, he would not have allowed me to make that run – Alex Ferguson would have coached him well – but I got into a good position when the ball came over.

'Wee Tam flighted the ball perfectly and, as I rose to meet it, I sensed that I would score. I met the ball straight on and headed it into the corner of the net with perfect weight. I can still remember the look on goalkeeper Bobby Clark's face as I met the ball. He knew that he couldn't get to the ball and that it was going into the net. It was a look of despair.

'The final whistle went shortly afterwards and we went up to pick up the Cup. It was Derek Johnstone's first as captain of Rangers and John Greig's first as manager, I recall. Afterwards we headed back to the stadium then headed off to Alex MacDonald's home in Kirkintilloch for a party. It was a great night and most of us stayed over, sleeping on the carpets and anywhere we could get some space.

'It was a great experience for me, scoring not only the winner but in the ninety-first minute when I knew my goal had won the Cup. It was strange that just a minute earlier I could not see a thing out of my eye, but by the time I scored I had a perfect view that would remain firmly imprinted in my mind for evermore.'

It was not the last trophy that Colin Jackson won at Rangers, but it was certainly a cup that carried more significance for him than most. The ecstasy of the Cup final was in contrast to the despair he suffered in the League two months later, when an own goal five minutes from time in the last game of the season set Celtic on their way to victory and the Championship. Rangers completed a Cup double with a win over Hibs to draw a close on a season which almost sealed a Treble for Greig. It was also one of mixed emotions for Colin Jackson, but he will always have special memories of the dramatic winner in the League Cup final.

AT THAT TIME

The Chrysler car plant at Linwood was in the news as a dispute brought production to an end.

On television, *Robin's Nest* was ITV's best comedy offering while on BBC Terry Wogan continued with the popular *Blankety Blank*.

Petrol prices were poised for a 4p rise to 89p.

In Pakistan, former President Bhutto was hanged.

The Eurovision Song Contest was won by an Israeli band, Milk and Honey.

Colin Jackson celebrated his award as Scottish Football Personality of the Month.

Colin Jackson in typical action for Rangers.

GEORGE BOWIE

To the avid listeners of Clyde 1, the nation's top-rated radio station, George Bowie is a disc jockey with musical interests that extend from Robbie Williams through Westlife to Madonna, but get him on to the subject of football and his affection for – er – Morton shines through! Yes, he has a soft spot for the team from the tail-of-the-bank, but he will not deny that he also has a strong affiliation to Rangers. Thankfully for Bowie, his true allegiances are rarely tested as the teams play in different leagues nowadays, but his bond with Rangers has strengthened over the years since he has taken part in the half-time match day entertainment and occasional duties behind the Public Address system.

Work at Ibrox has become as much a pleasure as a duty for the likeable Bowie. It gives him the opportunity to meet many of the players he has revered over the years and provides him with an insight into the workings of a major football ground. However, like the name of the Rangers 'Rising Stars' raffle that he hosts trackside each match day, Bowie has already began to fulfil the immense promise he showed when he first appeared on the airwaves. His career has taken him into Clyde's top slot in the breakfast show with over 750,000 listeners in the morning. In radio entertainment terms it is the Premier League and he is at the top. Williams, Kylie Minogue and even Britain's Prime Minister Tony Blair are regular visitors to the studio, although he is no less excited when he meets Advocaat, Amoruso and De Boer.

He was never going to be good enough to play for Rangers and, with his father an impresario and the family long involved in the entertainment business, it always seemed that his future lay more in that direction. However, he now has the best of both worlds.

EUROPEAN CHAMPIONS LEAGUE – QUALIFYING ROUND

RANGERS 2 (Vidmar, Reyna) PARMA 0

Attendance: 49,263

Ibrox Stadium, Glasgow – 11 August 1999

RANGERS: Klos; Porrini, Moore, Amoruso, Vidmar, Reyna, Ferguson, van Bronckhurst, McCann, Wallace and Mols.

PARMA: Buffon; Sartot, Thuram, Cannavaro, Serena, Boghossian, Walem, Baggio, Vanoli, Ortega and Di Vaio.

The Champions League campaign provides some mixed memories for George Bowie. For the visit of FC Haka of Finland he went along to Ibrox with his father, Ross Bowie, who was a long-time supporter and had close associations with many of the Rangers players of the past. It was a good night for Rangers as they sailed through the match, but it turned out to be a tragic night for George. Later that evening his father died of a massive heart attack.

George said, 'It really was the way to go, just as he would have wished it – taking in a Rangers game and then dying peacefully in his sleep.

'Regular match day announcer and good friend at Clyde, Bill Smith was due to go on holiday and had earlier asked me if I would take over for the next Champions League match. When my dad died he called to say that he would arrange for someone else to do it if I didn't feel up for it. I told him I would be okay and that I was looking forward to the game – we had drawn Parma in the next round.

'Ironically, I wasn't sure if I would be asked to do it again! I had taken over from Bill before, but in the last game I had covered, against Motherwell, I had nearly ended up in trouble! Bill had told me in the past that there was a dummy switch that ensured that the microphone was only live when the switch was pressed. It was straightforward enough, but he didn't tell me it had been changed before the Motherwell game.

'We went behind in that game and Paul Gascoigne was on the bench. I turned to someone in the PA box and said: "What the hell is Walter Smith thinking about with Gazza on the bench. He should be out there playing." Unfortunately, my observations were blasted out around the stadium. I got a quick call from secretary Campbell Ogilvie and that was that. I thought

I might never be asked again, although I don't think most people caught what I said.

'So when the opportunity arose again, I was desperate to do the job. Just after the draw was made my wife Ellen told me that she had had a dream that Rangers would be drawn against Parma and that we would beat them to go through. She had phoned up the bookmakers and was offered odds of 40/1 so she went straight down and put £40 on it. I went mental when I found out – I couldn't believe that she had done that on the basis of a dream. However, when the draw paired us with Parma, I started to wonder.

'On the night of the game I stopped off at the supermarket to buy Tina Turner's *Greatest Hits* CD. Rangers had stopped playing "The Best" at that time, but I took it along with a few other bits of music from my own collection. When I arrived, I was told that Dick Advocaat wanted me to gee up the fans. So as the kick-off neared I played "The Best" and told the fans that Advocaat wanted them to get right behind the team. The response was amazing. I was pretty nervous, but it was nothing to do with the PA – I speak to thousands over the radio each day – it was sheer adrenaline about the importance of the game.'

Parma were a strong side. In defence they had the elegant Thuram alongside respected Italian international defender Cannavaro. In the midfield their inspiration came from the dynamic Ortega who would contest the central area with Rangers' Barry Ferguson. Advocaat played a back four with Moore and Amoruso at the heart of the defence, with Rod Wallace and Michael Mols charged with the responsibility of breaking down the Italian defence.

'Any time I have been in the PA box the noise is muffled by the glass, but on this occasion it was deafening, especially when we opened the scoring through Vidmar. I was focused on the job, but I was also concentrating on the game. I was completely immersed in it – what an atmosphere it was.

'We got a second goal through Reyna and the whole place went wild. It was such an incredible feeling and I felt part of it all. The game ended 2–0 for Rangers and everyone was obviously delighted. There was no mention of the fact that I had played "The Best". In fact, I still have that CD in my collection.

'Of course the result took the possibility of my wife's dream coming true a little closer. We did eventually go on to get the result we needed in Italy and Ellen gleefully went down to the bookmakers to pick up her £1,600 winnings.

'The Champions League had begun on a sad note for me with my dad's death, but it also brought a really memorable match for me in the next round. I often reflect that my father went the way he would have wished, and that was some sort of comfort. The light began shining for me again though that evening against Parma – a truly memorable night.'

AT THAT TIME

The news was dominated by international concerns as India and Pakistan fought skirmishes over disputed territory.

In England, Aston Villa were top of the English Premiership, while Roy Keane deliberated over contract talks with Manchester United.

In golf, American Ryder Cup captain, Ben Crenshaw, slammed his players as speculation mounted that they wanted paid for playing at Brookline, Boston.

The world watched as a solar eclipse cast an eerie shadow over the northern hemisphere.

There were reports of Russia acting to try to stamp out Islamic fundamentalist uprisings in Chechnya.

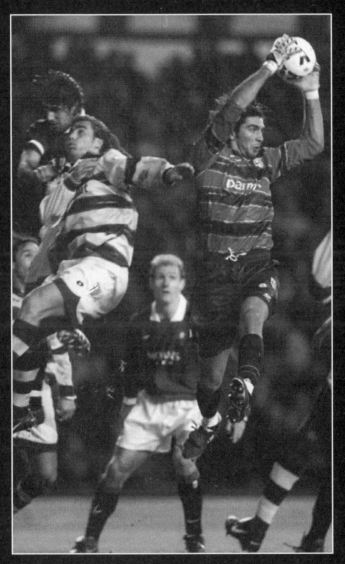

Gordon Durie waits for a slip from the Parma keeper Buffon.

ALAN McLAREN

Alan McLaren blossomed as a tough-tackling young full-back at Heart of Midlothian before moving into the centre of the defence where his performances captured the attention of a number of clubs, including Rangers. As Walter Smith looked to bolster his defence, he struck a deal with the Tynecastle side that saw Dave McPherson go eastwards as part of the transfer that took McLaren to Ibrox. The player swap aside, Rangers parted with £1.27 million as Smith signalled his intentions to strengthen the club's pursuit of the 'Nine-in-a-Row'.

McLaren settled quickly into the side, gaining his baptism in the cauldron of an Old Firm clash at Hampden, the temporary home of Celtic. The young defender played with immense spirit and resolve to show that he had the temperament to handle the tough schedule that the club would undoubtedly face in the coming months. Rangers won that clash with Celtic 3–1 and McLaren was a permanent fixture throughout the remainder of the season.

In the next season he played in every League match as Rangers won their eighth successive Championship, and he became a solid part of the side that sealed the historic ninth title at Tannadice Park, Dundee. However, he was becoming increasingly frustrated by injury and in 1998 heard the news that every player fears – that he would be unable to continue playing. At 27, it was a cruel blow for a player who had already achieved a lot, but promised so much more.

When he finally hung up his boots he had played almost 100 games for Rangers, winning the two League Championships and one Scottish Cup medal. He also won 24 caps for Scotland.

After a spell in Rangers Commercial Department, he left to set up business in his hometown of Edinburgh.

SCOTTISH PREMIER LEAGUE CHAMPIONSHIP
RANGERS 3 (Gascoigne 3) ABERDEEN 1 (Irvine)
Attendance: 47,250
Ibrox Stadium, Glasgow — 28 April 1996

RANGERS: Goram; Steven, Robertson, Gough, McLaren, Brown, Durie, Gascoigne, Andersen (McCoist), McCall and Laudrup.
ABERDEEN: Watt; McKimmie, Smith, Rowson, Irvine, Inglis, Bernard, Windass, Booth, Dodds and Glass.

Despite injury prematurely ending his career, Alan McLaren was fortunate to play in one of the most important periods in Rangers' history and alongside some of the best players to have filled the Light Blue jersey. His arrival coincided with the club's quest for the nine successive titles which became less of a dream and more of a reality as the titles mounted. He arrived with six on the trot already bagged, and there was a growing pressure on the club to complete the sequence. McLaren was just the kind of player whose grit and steely determination would be vital to the challenge. In his first season he helped Rangers negotiate the seventh Championship. With Brian Laudrup, Paul Gascoigne, Richard Gough and Ally McCoist, there was every chance that Rangers would complete the nine — and they did, in style.

Inevitably, the last three Championships carried some special memories for the young defender, but there was one above all others that proved more poignant. Alan McLaren had little hesitation in announcing his match to remember and the date of the game! 'Rangers against Aberdeen on 28 April 1996,' he said without a pause. 'It was a very special time for me because two days earlier, on 26 April, my wife gave birth to my daughter Ellie. She was our first child. We had a big game coming up against Aberdeen, knowing that a win would give us the Championship. But because of the birth, I was given the day off before the game. As a result I didn't train on either the Friday or the Saturday before the match, which was scheduled to be played on the Sunday afternoon.

'When I arrived at the stadium, I was obviously on a real high after the arrival of the baby and also knowing that a victory would give us the eighth championship. I felt good about the game and with people like Gascoigne and Laudrup in the side you have to be confident. However, Aberdeen got the first goal through Brian Irvine and I thought that the whole occasion might go pear-shaped for us. But I quickly got over that and then never really felt that we would not win.

'Gazza pulled us level when he jinked into the left of the box and scored from a tight angle. We were really on top at that stage and it seemed just a matter of time. Then I got in a header and it came off the woodwork. I thought that if it had gone in it would have completed a special day for me. But going into the second half, although we were still on top, the game was drifting and we still needed a goal. Gazza had worked really hard as usual, running up and down the field, and I could see he was tiring. I patted him on the side of the shorts and said, "Gazza, we need something, give us something special."

'He picked the ball up in our half then broke forward. Even though he was tired, the adrenaline and his sheer strength carried him through some hefty challenges. He brushed off Paul Bernard who chased him all the way and as he advanced on goal he coolly picked his spot, sending the ball inside Aberdeen keeper Michael Watt's left post. It was a magnificent goal. Gazza later claimed that I had jumped on him in the celebrations and winded him – cheeky Geordie b******, but I didn't! I stayed inside my own half.

'Later we got a penalty and, uncharacteristically, Ally McCoist handed it to Gazza. He scored to complete his hat-trick.

'The game finished 3–1 and that was enough to give us our eighth title. We stayed inside the stadium and had a bit of a party as you might expect, and then I headed back through to Edinburgh and up to the Eastern General Hospital. It turned out that my wife had watched the game on the television. It was only when I got there that the whole thing started to catch up with me and I found it hard to stay awake. It was just the sheer excitement of all that had gone on during these three days.

'When I look back on it, I think about the two chances I had – one in each half – when I hit the woodwork on both occasions. If they had gone in, it might have been "McLaren's Game" instead of Gazza's, but I don't begrudge him it. He had enormous influence on the game. And in any case I had my daughter and a Cup final to look forward to, coincidentally against my old team Hearts a few days later. It was a special period.'

McLaren did indeed play in the Cup final as Rangers romped to a 5–1 win. On that occasion, Laudrup was the star, scoring two goals to add to a hat-trick from Gordon Durie. It was a great era for Rangers and the next season was to provide further happiness for the side with the ninth title, although McLaren was not to know that his career was drawing to a close.

AT THAT TIME

The news was dominated by Britain's crippling BSE crisis and the German Premier added controversy by eating Scottish beef at a lunch while still maintaining his country's insistence on a UK export ban.

In football, Jim Leishman celebrated Livingston's promotion from the Third Division.

In England, Manchester United took a step closer to the title, beating Notts Forest 5–0.

On television Philip Schofield offered big prizes on *Talking Telephone Numbers* while Mike Smith fronted the more modest *That's Showbusines*.

Pop group Oasis gave fans in Manchester a super show with the promise of more to come at their concert at Loch Lomond in August.

Alan McLaren celebrates with Ally McCoist in the Ibrox
dressing-room after the win that gave them Rangers'
eighth successive title.

KAI JOHANSEN

When Bobby Shearer retired from Ibrox, Rangers struggled to fill the right-back berth, switching left-back Davie Provan into the role or others patently not suited to the position. Aware of his deficiencies in that area of the pitch, manager Scot Symon took the short trip down the Clyde to Greenock where Morton boss Hal Stewart had assembled a few Scandinavian players who were making their mark on the Scottish game. Among them was Kai Johansen, a Danish international who was already highly respected on the continent. Symon secured Johansen's signature for just £20,000 in the summer of 1965.

Johansen's arrival at Ibrox coincided with the rise of Celtic under Stein and it took the 25-year-old defender a little time to adjust to the style of play at Ibrox. More of the modern full-back of today's game, Johansen had to adapt to the more defensive style adopted by the Rangers full-backs of the '60s. However, when both club and player adapted to their strengths, he became a vital member of the side.

His crowning success while at Ibrox came in the 1966 Scottish Cup final replay against Celtic when he scored the only goal of the game. It was to be his only Cup triumph at Ibrox as the team struggled to keep apace with Jock Stein's Celtic, but Johansen was a stalwart who quickly embraced the club. When he retired in 1970, he had played almost 240 games for the club and had earned 26 caps with Denmark.

A successful businessman with interests in Scotland, Denmark and South Africa, Johansen still maintains close ties in the game, once working as an agent. He continues to liaise closely with Rangers in identifying new talent, and remains as devoted to the club as anyone. However, he will be best remembered for the goal that brought the Scottish Cup back to Rangers.

RANGERS 1 (Johansen) CELTIC 0
Attendance: 96,862
Ibrox Stadium, Glasgow – 27 April 1966

RANGERS: Ritchie; Johansen, Provan, Greig, McKinnon, Millar,
Wilson, Watson, McLean, Johnston and Henderson.
CELTIC: Simpson; Craig, Gemmell, Murdoch, McNeill, Clark, Johnstone,
McBride, Chalmers, Auld and Hughes.

There cannot be another foreign player who holds a passion for Rangers as strong as Kai Johansen. Like many who come to Ibrox from far shores, he quickly embraced the club, but his depth of feeling for Rangers is remarkably strong, especially given that he served through one of the most difficult periods in the club's history. After a spell of adjustment to the Rangers style of play, he established himself in the number 2 jersey and fought gamely to reverse the growing dominance of Celtic in the late '60s.

It was a trend in Scottish football that was to see the demise of Scot Symon and then Davie White, but Johansen was unbowed. He was proud that he had helped Rangers to a European Cup Winners' Cup final and then there was that famous Scottish Cup final win in 1966. It was a magical moment in time for Johansen, when he achieved the dream of every player – to score the winner in a Cup final. That it was an Old Firm final just added to the occasion. It was no surprise, therefore, that this is the match he considers his most memorable. His recollections of the build-up to the game and the match itself remain vivid more than 35 years on.

He recalled, 'At that time we were under enormous pressure because Celtic, under Stein, had some fabulous players and we didn't really have much chance of doing anything in the League, but the Cup was different.

'We fought through to the Cup final against Celtic. I remember in the lead-up to the game I never really appreciated what it all meant until we played the first game at Hampden. But even so, about two weeks before the game there was already a tightness in my stomach thinking about it. Despite my efforts to put it out of my mind, it was always there through that fortnight.

'In the final week before the game I was on edge, arguing with friends and family. It was just the tension of the match, but I was sure that the same was happening with the Celtic players. I just wanted to be with my teammates all the time, training with them and just getting involved in the football. Everything was geared towards the match. I knew virtually the whole week that I would be playing. You can tell from the team talks, and it was good because it did help me focus. There is a lot to be said for that knowing that you are playing well in advance.

'I think we went to Turnberry, or maybe Largs, then headed to Hampden. When we got to the stadium, I just wanted to be alone in the dressing-room. Every player has his own ritual – some sitting quiet, some shouting or whatever – but I wanted just some peace to myself. I went out to look at the park, but by that time you just want to get on with the game.

'The first five minutes of the game is always important and I settled in well. After that you are aware of the spectators – and they are a major part of it all – but you don't hear them. It was easy settling in because I was quite young, but had some more experienced players like Jimmy Millar around me. They played for the blue jersey and they helped me. I felt a Ranger, but I really didn't realise what it meant until the replay a few days later, after the Saturday game ended in a 0–0 draw.

'Waiting these extra few days made the whole thing worse from a tension viewpoint, especially when you feel for the club as I and the others did. We felt as desperate to win as the fans on the terracing. Maybe we were a little lucky to get a replay, but it was so important to Rangers that we were determined to go out there again and do it for the club, fans, and everyone.

'Again I would be up against John Hughes, who I hadn't done that well against in the past. In fact, in our early clashes he had made a fool out of me, but in the last few games we had played I had started to really get him under control. It meant that when I moved forward, he had to track back to cover me. I knew that he had been instructed to follow me back into defence when I broke forward. So, with him watching me more than me having to track his movements forward, it gave me a bit more freedom to get forward.

'In the replay, the game swung from end to end and then, with 20 minutes to go, the ball came to me outside the Celtic box on the right. I knew when I hit it that it was going into the net. You just know these things as a player and I connected with the ball very well.

'I was swamped by the rest of my teammates and, as I lay on the ground, the wee man, Willie Henderson, picked me up and said, "Now, Kai, you know what it is to be a Ranger." I hadn't really appreciated what it all meant until that goal. Rangers is all about passion, the blue jersey, the traditions. If you don't have that passion about the game, you shouldn't be at a club like Rangers.

'What happened after that was indescribable. I really felt that I had graduated as a Rangers player. We travelled around the supporters' clubs at that time and that helped build the club in my heart. We didn't do it out of duty; we went because we wanted to go and meet the fans. They would pamper us, love us, and that was so important in building the bond between us. That was how I became a Ranger.

'After having a terrible start with the club, they became adapted to my style of play as an overlapping full-back and wee Willie learned to cover me when I went forward. Ironically, I asked Symon to let me leave early on because I thought I was making a fool of myself, but he changed the pattern to suit me. But I always had faith in my ability. I had been selected for the Europe XI in the Stanley Matthews Testimonial match and that really made me. I also won 26 caps, and the Cup final sometimes overshadows all of that. However, as a moment and an experience, there was nothing higher than playing against Celtic and scoring the winning goal in that Cup final.'

AT THAT TIME

In England, the Moors Trial of Brady and Hindley continued amidst huge public interest.

In the charts, Cher was in the No. 2 position with 'Bang, Bang'.

On television, *Emergency Ward 10* was popular with prime-time viewers.

In England, Tommy Docherty, manager of Chelsea, turned down a bid of £70,000 for Terry Venables.

A packet of 20 Kensitas cigarettes cost 5 shillings and 5 pence.

Kai Johansen at a private function surrounded
by well-wishers.

DOUGIE DONNELLY

Brought up in Rutherglen and with a grandfather who was a fervent supporter of the Clyde, it is only natural that Dougie Donnelly holds the 'Bully Wee' closest to his heart but, having produced two Rangers history videos, there is hardly a fan who knows more about the famous Ibrox club.

A star of television and radio, Donnelly may even have earned his living in a football jersey had an initial trial period at Shawfield proved more successful. A centre-half who was 'tall before his time', he quickly gave up notions of making it in the game at 17. Instead he went to Strathclyde University to study law, successfully going on to earn his degree.

It was while at university that he first dabbled as a disc jockey; he showed such ease over the microphone that he was snapped up by Radio Clyde and introduced to broadcasting. His progress to television was rapid, and in 1978 he delivered his first match report for the BBC in the inauspicious surroundings of Broomfield Park, Airdrie. By the end of the year he had moved into the studio and his first anchor role on BBC *Sportscene* came on a Wednesday evening when he introduced the highlights of Rangers' famous European Cup win over Juventus. It was a good evening, with all on the production team on a high as they brought the coverage of a good result for Scottish football.

Donnelly never looked back and he finished with Clyde in 1992 to concentrate on his increasing television workload. He calls himself a 'sports fan with a microphone', and his casual unflappable style has taken him into the cauldron of almost every major sporting arena to interview players from the highest levels in golf, snooker, bowling and, of course, football.

One of the most complete sports presenters in the game, his next winter Olympics will be his fifth. Then it will be the Masters and the Open – a glamorous tour of world sporting events. Through it all, however, he hasn't lost sight of his roots and still remains in Glasgow, taking in matches at Broadwood Stadium, where Clyde play, whenever he can. But he retains an affection for Rangers through his work on these history projects. The associations between the two clubs run deep. As he will tell you, two Rangers managers, Struth and White, served their apprenticeship at the Shawfield, but that is another story – get the video!

SCOTTISH LEAGUE CUP FINAL
RANGERS 3 (McCoist 3) CELTIC 2 (McClair, Reid)
Attendance: 66,369
Hampden Park, Glasgow – 25 March 1984

RANGERS: McCloy; Nicholl, Dawson; McClelland, Paterson, McPherson; Russell, McCoist, Clark (McAdam), MacDonald (Burns) and Cooper.
CELTIC: Bonner; McGrain, Reid; Aitken, McAdam, McLeod; Provan (Sinclair), P. McStay, McGarvey (Melrose), Burns and McClair.

A Cup final will inevitably provide a kaleidoscope of memories for players and fans alike. For the winners there is the glory of presentation with coloured ribbons cascading down the cup. For the losers there is the dream of what might have been as the fans filter away quietly. Fans of both sides of the Old Firm have experienced all the emotions of the game. They come to Hampden fervently hoping and often blindly convinced that there will be only one winner, although instinctively they know that only time will tell. For the neutral, detached from the intensity of the emotions of Cup final day, it is no more than a game. Ordinarily that is how Dougie Donnelly would have viewed the 1984 Cup final clash between Celtic and Rangers, but there were issues that focused his mind firmly on an Ibrox win on that occasion.

He recalled, 'I had been commissioned by Rangers to produce a history video entitled, *Follow, Follow*. At that time I was pretty friendly with John Greig, in fact it was John who wanted me to do the video. However, the team had really started to struggle under John. We just kept on working away, although we knew that John was under pressure. Then the project was put on hold as things didn't pick up on the field. Finally, in October, John Greig resigned to be replaced with Jock Wallace. It was very sad because John was a good friend and we all felt for him, but the project moved forward again. A lot of the filming took place over the winter of season 1983–84. I remember we did a lot of it in the boardroom at Ibrox with the likes of Jock Shaw, Willie Waddell, and George Young. However, we were looking for a good result to hang the whole project on. We were hoping that it might come in the Scottish Cup, but Rangers went out at the fifth-round stage to Dundee. It was a big shock and set everyone back. However, the team had fought through to the League Cup final with the match scheduled to be played a week later.

'I remember Ally McCoist had gone through a pretty rough time around about then and had taken some abuse from the Rangers fans. In fact, it may well have reached a peak in that Cup defeat by Dundee. I remember Derek Johnstone told me that he had told Ally to walk out of the stadium with his head held high as the crowd gathered around the front door of Ibrox.

'A couple of nights before the match I filmed a programme called *Connolly with Donnelly*, which featured Billy Connolly. After the show, Billy, who was a big Celtic fan, talked about how Celtic would see off Rangers and we had a bit of banter about that.

'When we got to Hampden, I had a film crew with me. It was fortunate that STV had live coverage that year because it freed me from my BBC duties to work on the project. It was the first time I felt really partisan in an Old Firm game and I have to say it was for mercenary reasons. We really needed a Rangers win for the video.

'The game turned out to be one of the most exciting finals in years, with Ally McCoist scoring the opener just after the break and then getting a second around the hour mark. However, Celtic fought back to level, with Mark Reid getting the equaliser right on the final whistle. The game went into extra-time and then, as Ally burst through towards the end of the first period, he was bundled over by Roy Aitken. It was a penalty, and in typical McCoist fashion he added to the drama by having his spot-kick first saved, before he knocked in the rebound. McCoist had completed his hat-trick and Rangers went on to hold on to the win.

'After the match we got access to the team bus as it made its way back to Ibrox. I remember there was a lot of singing and I have this image of assistant boss Alex Totten singing his heart out. Jimmy Nicholl and John McClelland, who was captain, were at the centre of it all. It was a tremendous experience for me and the film crew, being part of all that as the bus made its way along Paisley Road West, with fans lining the streets.

'When we got back to the ground we didn't hang around – we just wanted to let them get on with it – but we had what we needed. It helped to make the video and was important for us and the club. It was also something of a turning point for Ally McCoist. He never really looked back after that.'

Indeed, it was a turning point for McCoist and a boost for Jock Wallace in his return to Rangers. It seemed happier times were ahead for Rangers. For Donnelly the chances of Clyde ever reaching these heights seem increasingly remote, however.

AT THAT TIME

The news was dominated by turmoil in the coal industry as six of the country's biggest pits ceased production in the face of strike action.

In London, Barbra Streisand attended the premiere of her latest movie *Yentl*.

In football, Graeme Souness hit the winner as Liverpool beat Everton in the replay of the Milk Cup final.

On television, Colin Baker took up the role of *Doctor Who*.

For motorists, a Toyota Corolla cost £5,249.

A bottle of Whyte and Mackay whisky cost £6.89.

Hat-trick hero Ally McCoist clutches his
medal and the League Cup.

ARTUR NUMAN

Rangers fans watched the 1998 World Cup excitedly in the knowledge that Dutch star Artur Numan would come to Ibrox after the tournament was over. The first Dutchman to sign for Dick Advocaat at Rangers, the manager knew all about Numan – he was his captain at PSV Eindhoven. Advocaat had no hesitation in paying £4.5 million for the left-sided defender, who had the versatility to allow options for his selection in midfield.

Numan came to Ibrox with a solid career in Holland behind him and success already achieved at PSV Eindhoven. He won the Championship, Dutch Cup and Super Cup in a glorious spell that broke the domination of the traditionally strong Ajax and Feyenoord.

Rangers, however, offered him a new challenge and he settled in quickly at Ibrox, helping the side to the Treble in the first season, although his appearances were severely limited through injury. Indeed, it has only been in season 2001–02, when he finally got clear of his injury worries, that Rangers saw the real Numan – a player with striking pace and desire to get into attacking positions. A popular player who always has time for the fans, he has won two Championships, one Scottish Cup and one League Cup with Rangers. Capped over 40 times for Holland, he is a key member of Advocaat's side.

SCOTTISH CUP FINAL
ABERDEEN 0 RANGERS 4 (van Bronckhorst, Vidmar, Dodds, Albertz)
Attendance: 50,865
Hampden Park, Glasgow – 27 May 2000

ABERDEEN: Leighton (Winters), Whyte, Solberg, Anderson (Belabed), McAllister, Bernard, Jess, Rowson, Guntveit, Stavrum (Zerouali) amd Dow.
RANGERS: Klos, Reyna, Moore (Porrini), vidmar, Numan, Kanchelskis, Ferguson, Albertz, van Bronckhorst (Tugay), Wallace (McCann) and Dodds.

A rtur Numan's remarkable success in Holland with PSV Eindhoven did not diminish his joy when he first won a trophy for Rangers. The occasion was the League Cup final and the venue was Celtic Park where a stuffy St Johnstone side put up some resistance before Rangers took the game by two goals to one. Numan enjoyed the victory immensely. Having returned from the World Cup in France, disappointed, but with his considerable reputation further advanced, the Cup final win was a refreshing change for the Dutchman among his new teammates. Dick Advocaat had reconstructed the side from the outset and Numan, his captain at PSV, was his first signing.

Numan recalled when he first decided to come to Rangers, 'We were a family club at PSV, but what impressed me about Rangers was the friendliness of everyone. From the people on the board to the cleaning staff, kitchen ladies and groundstaff, everyone was so friendly. I immediately felt at home and put pen to paper on a four-year deal. I have in fact just extended that deal which confirms my feelings about the club.

'I enjoyed that first Cup final tremendously, but the one match which means even more to me was the Scottish Cup final against Aberdeen in 1999. We went through our usual preparation for the game, training on the day before the game then staying overnight at the hotel. The next morning, the manager ran through the team talk and announced the team. He told us about Aberdeen, but concentrated more on what we could bring to the game. It is always more important to focus on your own qualities.

'When we got to the ground, the chairman, David Murray, came downstairs to the dressing-room with Sean Connery to wish us good luck. It was a nice gesture and helped remove any nerves. I found it strange to think that I had watched Sean Connery in movies as a youngster and here he was in our dressing-room before a Cup final in Glasgow. I could never have imagined that would happen.

'I went out to the pitch for a warm-up and couldn't believe what I saw. Half of the ground was in red, for Aberdeen, but the rest was full of orange. It was a strange feeling because having played for Holland in European Championships and World Cups I was used to seeing the Dutch supporters like that, but not Rangers. It really felt like a Dutch international match. The atmosphere was incredible.

'They told us it was intended as a salute to the manager and the Dutch players, but we knew that there was perhaps a bit more to it than that. However, the atmosphere was fantastic and after the game I spoke to some friends I had over for the game, including the PSV keeper Ronald

Wattereus. They told me that when they got into the ground they had to ask the Rangers fans what was going on. They couldn't understand why everyone was in orange.

'Playing in that game gave me a special feeling and there were times that it felt as if I was playing for Holland. It was all the more special because I was captain that day.

'The game turned out quite easy for us after Jim Leighton got injured and was sent off in the first minute. It really became a bit of a procession after that, but I still thoroughly enjoyed it. It was a great time of course, because we had won the Championship too. But that final will always remain quite special to me because of the fans. They are so important to the game and when they are loud it particularly helps drive me on. As I stand in the tunnel, in the big games especially, I can feel the adrenaline flowing. The Rangers fans can really be the twelfth man in matches.

'That is how it was that day at Hampden and it really impressed my friends. They spoke of the unbelievable atmosphere in the stadium, and the mass of orange. It was a very special day.'

The Scottish Cup win was Numan's first at Hampden, injury having ruled him out of the win over Celtic that sealed the Treble a year earlier. Only time will tell if he can add to his already impressive collection of prizes, but one thing is certain – Hampden is unlikely to see scenes like those he experienced that fine day in 1999. It was a day when Scotland's national stadium could easily have seemed to be Holland's. Strangely, it helped Numan and his compatriots feel a little more at home. However, for the moment at least, home to Numan is Scotland.

AT THAT TIME

The news was dominated with reports that a suspect had been arrested in connection with the Jill Dando murder.

While Rangers celebrated their Cup victory, Celtic announced that Martin O'Neill would take over as their new boss. Meanwhile, Rangers were linked with Feyenoord defender Bert Konterman.

In music, Fran Healy and his band Travis celebrated two Ivor Novello awards.

The lead-up to the final was shrouded in controversy as Aberdeen protested at their ticket allocation.

In sport it was speculated that Mike Tyson and Lennox Lewis would battle it out for the heavyweight crown at Hampden – the fight never materialised.

Artur Numan proudly receives the Scottish
Cup for Rangers.